Raising
Worldly-Wise
But Innocent
Kids

Discovery House Publishers

Books, music, and videos that feed the soul with the Word of God

Box 3566 Grand Rapids, MI 49501

Raising Worldly-Wise But Innocent Kids

Wisdom from the Book of Proverbs for Modern Families

David Wyrtzen

Raising Worldly-Wise But Innocent Kids
Copyright © 1995 by David B. Wyrtzen

Discovery House Publishers is affiliated with RBC Ministries, Grand Rapids, Michigan 49512.

Discovery House books are distributed to the trade exclusively by Barbour Publishing, Inc., Uhrichsville, Ohio 44683.

All Scripture quotations, unless noted otherwise, are from the author's own translation.

Requests for permission to quote from this book should be directed to:
Permissions Department, Discovery House Publishers, P.O. Box 3566,
Grand Rapids, MI 49501

Library of Congress Cataloging-in-Publication Data

Wyrtzen, David, 1949–
    Raising worldly-wise but innocent kids: wisdom from the book of Proverbs/ by David Wyrtzen.
        p.   cm.
    Originally published: Chicago : Moody Press, © 1990.
        ISBN 1-57293-002-0
        1. Child rearing—United States. 2. Child rearing—Religious
        aspects. I. Title
    [HQ769.W97   1995]
    248.8'45—dc20   95-31586
                                                                          CIP

Printed in the United States of America

05 06 07 08 09 10 11 / CHG / 11 10 9 8 7 6 5 4

To my dad, Jack Wyrtzen,
who was my example of a wise father
on his knees before God each morning
with the sacred Scriptures,

and to my Hebrew teacher, Bruce Waltke,
who gave me not only exegetical tools
but the example of a life filled with passion—
passion to study the Hebrew text
and to bring it to life in the marketplace.

Contents

Acknowledgments   viii
Foreword   ix

Introduction   1

The Designer: A Father with a Skillful Plan for Living

1. A Wise Head on Young Shoulders   13
2. Respect the Architect   27
3. The Demolition Crew   41
4. Follow the Instructions   61

Money Blueprints

5. Bonnie and Clyde   75
6. The Sting   91
7. The Sluggard   103
8. Skillful Money Management   111

Sex Blueprints

9. The Sex Teacher   125
10. The Seductress   135
11. Preventatives and Cures   147
12. The Intoxicating Wife   159
13. God's Liberated Woman   167

Leadership Blueprints

14. The Spiked Punch Bowl   183
15. Word Power   191
16. God and Power Politics   199

Conclusion   213

Acknowledgments

My students at the Word of Life Bible Institute, my church family of over twenty years in Midlothian, Texas, and above all my four children, Jonathan, Joel, Joshua, and Jenae, gave me the opportunity to see the power of the ancient text of Proverbs transform lives today. Without them this book would be lifeless. And without my faithful ally at my side this book could not have been written. Thanks, Mary, for your heart and your encouragement.

I am also indebted to Robert K. DeVries and the gifted editorial staff at Discovery House for believing enough in the reality of the learn-and-live philosophy of parenting to keep these principles in print. Thanks to all my friends at Discovery House.

Foreword

Many summers ago, my wife, Jill, and I were regular attenders at Word of Life Bible Camp at Schroon Lake, New York. We always looked forward to the outstanding weeks of Bible training and spiritual leadership we received there. It was during one of those summers that young David Wyrtzen crossed our path.

Our immediate response was that this young man could not teach us anything new. It soon became evident, however, that he had much to share from the book of Proverbs. Under his instruction, the ancient proverbs came alive. He breathed a new freshness into them and imparted a vitality and meaningfulness that we had never before experienced.

Jill and I used to wish that we could have all of the life applications from Proverbs in book form that we could use in our personal study and also share with our eighteen kids. You can imagine how excited we were when we learned that Dave Wyrtzen's unique insights into Proverbs were finally going to be published.

I am delighted that Dave has written this practical, much-needed book. This kind of treatment is long overdue. After you finish reading this remarkable book, I'm sure you will agree with me that the book of Proverbs has never been more alive and more ably applied to the challenging task of raising our kids to face real life.

Three cheers for Dave Wyrtzen . . . and for King Solomon!

Pat Williams
General Manager, Orlando Magic, NBA
Coauthor of the bestselling *Rekindled*

Introduction

Parenting the Intel®, Microsoft® generation is intimidating. When I compete against my kids in video games, I become painfully aware of this reality. It's humbling for me to lose to my teenagers Joshua and Jenae in a Nintendo® game. It's more humbling to realize that my sons and daughter learn in elementary school what I learned in college. State-of-the-art media flashes before their eyes everything from the gyrating seductiveness of MTV to CNN's live broadcasts of the bombing of Sarajevo. Communication tools have never been faster or more pervasive. Therefore, the computer generation has an air of technical sophistication. But do they have a clearer grasp of spiritual realities or moral standards? Does their broadened exposure through the media and quicker adaptation to new technology guarantee that they have a clearer idea of how to live a wise life?

A scan of the latest headlines—"Kids Killing Kids," "Drive-by Shooting Takes Teen Life," "AIDS Invades Heterosexual Relationships," "Children of Divorce"—reveals that advances in technology may have exploded, but morality marches relentlessly in the opposite direction. A *Time* headline once asked "What Ever Happened to Ethics—Assaulted by Sleaze, Scandals and Hypocrisy, America Searches for Its Moral Bearings" (May 25, 1987).

Many still search as we begin the twenty-first century. Moral bearings—they are as needed in daily life as an accurate heading indicator is needed by an airline pilot, but computer chips cannot provide the right moral directions. What are dads and moms supposed to do in a society where powerful media preachers are caught sleeping with prostitutes while moneyed Wall Street brokers go to jail for acting illegally on inside information? No won-

1

der we feel defensive as parents and wish there were some way we could isolate our children from the seductive influences seeking to destroy them.

As a father of four I personally feel this intense desire to protect my kids from all the immorality, deception, substance abuse, and violence of contemporary America. Sometimes I dream of locking them up in a monastery where they would be safe.

The Monastery Parent

When I counsel parents I find that many of them identify with my feelings of wanting to isolate our kids from the influence of the secular world system. I refer to this child-raising philosophy as monastery parenting. Fred and Mary represent this type of parent. In their college days during the sixties they rode the flower-child wave of Vietnam War protest, sit-ins, and marches to fulfill the dream of civil rights for all. But assassins' bullets, drug overdoses, and venereal diseases caused them to question the assumptions behind the Age of Aquarius. In the midst of their search for meaning a friend challenged them to reconsider the claims of the most influential Person in world history. Through reading His story in the fourth book of the New Testament they both decided to trust Jesus Christ. He did give them a new life, but their past makes them painfully aware of consequences of sin. They know the scars and they fear for their eight- and ten-year-olds.

Over coffee in their living room Fred shares his concerns. "I thought things were coming apart in the sixties. But it has gotten worse. Last night Lance asked me if they had crack when I was growing up. And last Friday he brought home a piece of paper covered with occult pentagrams. One of his classmates told him these were only nice designs. I fear for my kids and I intend to protect my family by creating a totally Christian environment. The rules about dress, music, and entertainment will be strict. I'll make sure they never come in contact with the influences that seduced me. I'm going to build a wall around my children which will guarantee that no corrupting influences can pollute their innocent minds."

I empathize with Fred and Mary's concern. Our children are vulnerable, and our job as parents is to protect them. But can we defeat evil by isolation? Will turning back the clock to the days of *Father Knows Best* and *Leave It to Beaver* conquer evil's internal as well as external assault against our kids? Is ignorance really bliss? Too often I have to listen to the cries of monastery parents when the reality of evil has scaled their protective walls.

"We attended a Gospel-preaching, Bible-teaching church, but now what do we do? Our fifteen-year-old is pregnant."

"Our kids were never allowed to touch a drop! How could our John be on the hospital detox floor trying to conquer alcoholism?"

"We sent Debbie to a good Christian college. How could she just move in with her boyfriend and be so cold concerning spiritual things?"

"Every Sunday our pastor screamed against perversion. He could not possibly have been having affairs with so many women."

Whether our kids are home-schooled, Christian-schooled, or public-schooled, we must all face the fact that nostalgic reruns from the fifties will not equip us or our children to overcome the sophisticated temptations of today. We cannot turn back the clock and long for the days when morality was as American as apple pie and Chevrolets. The wise realist of Ecclesiastes warns us against yearning for the good old days: "Do not say, 'Why were the old days better than these?' It is not wise to ask such questions" (7:10).

In reality the monastery philosophy was already thoroughly tested in the good old days. It failed!

The first-century Pharisees were Super Bowl champions at trying to conquer temptation by isolationism and rigid rules. They critically attacked Jesus because His disciples did not honor the traditions passed down by their learned religious teachers (Mark 7:5)—traditions skillfully designed to erect a wall around the moral law of God so that human passions could be controlled and the individual kept safe from yielding to evil. Jesus' reply to these religionists reveals the internal inconsistency whenever any of us tries to generate morality by locking individuals in an external behavior pattern. He exposes the fatal fallacy of this approach. It fails because it attempts to clean up internal moral filth with an external bath. Listen carefully to His analysis.

> Isaiah was right when he prophesied about you hypocrites; as it is written: "These people honor me with their lips, but their hearts are far from me. They worship me in vain; their teachings are but rules taught by men" (Mark 7:6–7 NIV).

The monastery philosophy of raising children cannot generate a deep intimacy with God which alone can yield a wise, moral lifestyle. It mislocates the problem of evil in external influences rather than in an internal condition. Walls cannot be built high enough to keep evil away from our kids. It has already infected their insides. The isolationist technique is an impotent religious tradition which can never handle the virility of evil. Jesus labeled this legalism *stupidity!*

> Are you so dull? . . . Don't you see that nothing that enters a man from the outside can make him "unclean"?

. . . . For from within, out of men's hearts, come evil thoughts, sexual immorality, theft, murder, adultery, greed, malice, deceit, lewdness, envy, slander, arrogance and folly. All these evils come from inside and make a man "unclean" (Mark 7:18, 21–23 NIV).

We must not repeat the same foolish mistake of the first-century Pharisees. When they rooted evil in material things, they mislocated the enemy and they overestimated the power of their external rules to control this evil within. Evil is not outside. It is inside the human heart. It is a deadly moral virus that has infected every human heart. Isolationism and rules cannot cure it. Children raised in monastery-style environments where devotion to God is equivalent to attending church services, giving a few coins in the offering, memorizing Bible verses, and having the right haircut, never face the danger that lurks within and the power of God to perform a moral heart transplant.

These religious kids, without an authentic intimacy with God, tend to grow up with an overpowering passion to escape from all the rigidity. Usually their rebellion causes them to naively experiment with evil. When they marry and have children, they vow their home will be free from the slavery of religious tradition. Their children will be free to discover their own standards and spiritual values. Thus, in reaction to rigid monastery-style parenting the pendulum swings in the home, as it does in society, from too much control to too much permissiveness.

The Laissez-faire Parent

Laissez-faire is a philosophy that deliberately abstains from giving direction. Noninterference and a stress on individual freedom of choice and action govern its policies. When applied to parenting, it means to refrain from inhibiting a child's creative self-development. Never give them authoritative guidance in spiritual and moral matters. Charlene and Frank illustrate this approach to raising kids.

Charlene's dad is the pastor of a large fundamentalist church. In her teen years she rebelled, ran away from home, and got pregnant. A year-long marriage to the father of her child proved disastrous. Now at twenty-eight she is married to a successful attorney and her career in interior design has taken off. During a quick lunch between appointments she shares with me some of her thoughts about raising her own family.

"Frank and I trust our children. We want them to experiment and follow their instincts. Why not let them have their fling? After all, in spite of my dad's multitude of sermons, I sowed my wild oats. All that church attendance and Bible reading my parents subjected me to didn't keep me from getting in trouble. My children will have the right to discover their own personal meaning without my interference. At least they are not growing up in all that pious hypocrisy."

I asked Charlene if I could share a challenge my wife and I faced in teaching our daughter Jenae the meaning of the word *hot* when she was two. She nodded.

"We use a wood-burning stove to heat our home. When cranked up, its surface temperature peaks about 1000 degrees. As Jenae reached the crawling, I'm-into-everything stage, Mary came to me and was concerned.

" 'Dave, if Jenae plants her little palm on that stove, she will be scarred for life!'

"My masculine laissez-faire response was, 'That'll teach her! She'll never touch hot stoves again.'

"Charlene, do you really believe this was my approach to teaching Jenae about hot stoves? What kind of parents would allow their toddler to learn about hot stoves by trial-and-error experimentation?" She grimaced at the thought of Jenae's charred palm. "Yet you just told me this was your approach when it comes to the far more serious moral and spiritual dangers your children will face."

The laissez-faire parent naively forgets that the school of experience is efficient, but cruel. A grotesque scarred palm is too high a price to pay to learn the meaning of the word *hot*. The deaths of thousands of teenagers is too high a cost to learn that the illicit use of drugs is wrong. Becoming the victim of AIDS or giving birth to an illegitimate baby is too high a price for a lesson in the advantages of sexual purity. The learn-by-experience, do-your-own-thing approach was popular in the sixties, but in the nineties we must wise up to its wreckage of human lives. So where do we go from here? What is an effective parental training model for the beginning of the twenty-first century? How should our children learn about the hot spots in life?

Learn-and-Live Parenting

When Mary faced me with the danger posed by our red-hot stove, I immediately contacted a skilled welder. He built a large metal screen around the stove so that Jenae could not get near the searing surface. We then began an intense course in the meaning of *hot*. I took her by the hand and brought her near the stove where she could feel the heat. "Hot! Hot!" We repeated, "Hurt, Jenae! Ow! Don't touch!" This approach arose from our genuine love for our daughter, our personal conviction concerning the danger of hot stoves, and our effectiveness in teaching her these realities. While she was too little to understand, the protective metal screen was needed. But now it has been removed. It is no longer necessary. Jenae matured to the point where she decided for herself that it was foolish to get burned by insisting on planting her five chubby fingers on the hot stove. In this case she accepted our love and the reality of our teaching about the pain of burned flesh, and the palm of her hand remains beautiful. Learn-and-live parenting provides strong protective rules while children are young, but its goal is to progressively explain the "whys" for the standards, so that when the children leave home, they are young adults who have personally internalized the life of godly wisdom.

Today's younger generation needs adults who will love them enough to point out where the hot spots in life are, to be tough enough to build authoritative fences to protect them from these dangers while they are immature, and to invest the personal time necessary to progressively train teenagers how to make right ethical choices on their own. Our lives must demonstrate the happiness found in living wisely. We must stop coveting our teenager's youth and fully accept our adult responsibility to teach the next generation how to live. But where do we find the correct principles for living?

Though dusty with age and far removed from the *New York Times'* bestseller list, the Old Testament book of Proverbs is still the ultimate parental training manual. These proverbs appear to be quaint, old-fashioned relics of a bygone era or obvious trivialities anyone should know. But when mined with perseverance they prove to be nuggets glistening with life's realities.

Proverbs is a gutsy book about money, sex, and power. It exposes the con-game of the drug pusher, the seduction of the prostitute, and the sarcasm of an agnostic university professor. It does not blush when talking about the intimacies of sexual love, or shrink from the evolutionist's challenge concerning the creation. Most importantly it reveals God's personal philosophy of child-rearing.

He chooses neither the protectionism of the monastery nor the experimentation of the laissez-faire method. Instead He penetrates deep inside our children's personalities and challenges them with the choices in life which will bring success and those that will yield disaster. He courts them to decide to love, trust, and respect Him. He advises them to be worldly wise but to remain innocent—wise as a snake concerning evil's allure but pure as a dove concerning involvement in sin. His top priority is an invitation. He desires to live inside their personalities and give them the power, not only to know the right decision, but also to make the right choice.

Will our children be able to say that their dad and mom loved them enough to teach them, not just how to make a living, but how to live? When our children leave the shelter of our homes will they be sheltered by the wisdom only God can teach them?

For me these are not theoretical issues. Mary and I are in the midst of raising three sons and a daughter. Just yesterday, it seems, I waited nervously in the waiting room (it was back when dads were not welcome in the delivery room) while Mary gave birth to our oldest. When I wrote the first edition of this book, Jonathan was asking me to teach him to drive. Now he and his brother Joel are in college. Josh and Jenae are both teenagers. Our parenting days are moving at the speed of light. So will yours. Will we use the speeding moments to train each of our children in God's school of skillful living? Or will they have to be scarred in the school of hard knocks?

My purpose in writing is to share the facts about life that God is teaching us from Proverbs, to share how our family is struggling to apply the learn-and-live approach to parenting in the computer age, and to learn together how not to send our kids to the school of hard knocks. Since the first edition of this book our two older boys have grown up and gone out into the world. By God's graciousness, so far they have chosen wisely. Mary and I now know by experience that kids can be raised without being destroyed in the school of hard knocks. They can leave our homes prepared to go out to invade the secular society with the powerful truth that Jesus Christ is alive. If you want to learn how to raise this kind of godly child—kids who can go out to invade and transform a god-less world—then these pages are for you.

The first step in generating this kind of young person is to find a "Dr. Spock" who will tell us the truth about raising kids; some-one whose advice will not become obsolete when the next best-seller tops the charts.

Think About It

1. When you send your kids away to college or a career, what objectives do you hope to have accomplished in their lives? Write these objectives down and discuss them with your spouse.

2. How did your parents impart values to you? Where did they suc-ceed? Where did they fail? How is your parental pattern a reaction to your upbringing?

3. What is the dominant parental philosophy of your home? Monastery philosophy? Laissez-faire? Learn-and-live? How do you as husband and wife differ in philosophy?

4. Think of a situation where you as parents did train one of your children in a life reality with the goal to help him or her become skillful in making these decisions independently. How did your child respond? Why is this approach difficult?

5. Who are the authorities you are depending upon to give you the right information about child rearing? How have their children turned out? Why did the apostle Paul counsel that elders in churches needed to be fathers who had demonstrated skill in rais-ing their children (1 Timothy 3:4–5)? Could you interact with a mature couple in your church about raising kids? Why not set up a dinner date and have them over?

The Designer:
A Father with a
Skillful Plan for Living

Intimacy with the Creator
is the greatest gift we can give our children.

1

A Wise Head on Young Shoulders

Super catch, Gary! Trying to tackle me?" The senior wide-receiver was relieved that Cathy, one of the cheerleaders, could still talk. He had managed to hold on to the football but knocked her flat when he tumbled out of bounds. "Sorry! You okay? Their defensive cornerback tried to plant me in the stands. I'll tell our quarterback to stay away from the sideline pass, but at least I made the catch and a first down!"

"I guess this cheerleading gets dangerous at times," she laughed.

Gary returned to join his team in the huddle but not before he took another glance toward the sideline. Cathy's smile, waist-length blond hair, and slim figure could turn any football player's head.

A spectator glancing down at these two East Texas High School teenagers could easily conclude that their lives would have charmed destinies. Physically attractive, intellectually gifted, socially desirable—success? They couldn't miss! Graduation day thrust these seniors upon the serious path of adult life—a path that took them to completely different destinations, for only one was prepared for the trip.

Cathy decided she needed some practical exposure to the nine-to-five world of business before furthering her education. The Dallas-Fort Worth Metroplex invited her to the land of opportunity. Her parents were reluctant but when Susan, a long-time friend of the family, moved up to the Metroplex from Austin, Mom and Dad gave in. The new roommates moved into an apartment and made plans to take on the world.

Dressed smartly in her tailored suit, Cathy's "cover-girl" look landed her a job in no time as a receptionist in North Dallas. The money was just fair, but the social life was magnificent. Susan tried to interest Cathy in a career class at a church near their apartment, but she couldn't help thinking how boring these get-togethers were compared to the clubs Joan was introducing her to.

Joan was the boss's secretary. Sophisticated and fun, she knew the right clothes, nightspots, and men. Cathy never dreamed life could be so fast and free.

"Tony Bennett is doing the Venetian Room at the Fairmont Friday night, Cathy. I'll pick you up at your place at seven." Thirty, successful, and smooth, Mick Johnson was confident with women. Running into him in the hall after returning from a coffee break caught Cathy by surprise, but she managed to blurt out, "Yes, Mick, that sounds like fun."

To a nineteen-year-old, Tony Bennett was boring, but with Mick even a piano recital could be scintillating. Susan nagged her with questions about Mick's character. Cathy felt she was living with her mother again instead of with an eighteen-year-old roommate.

The girls in the office teased her all week about her date with the new man in town. But in the soft, dim light of the Venetian Room Friday evening the men could not stop glancing at the petite girl in the romantic lace cocktail dress. Mick did not tease.

He refilled Cathy's wine glass and tenderly took her hand. He mentioned his hotel room quietly but with confidence. This was a far cry from the bumbling high school boys she had dated. The wine was sweet and his touch was slow and reassuring. With Tony

Bennett love ballads filling her mind, Cathy spent her first night in bed with a man.

Saturday morning when she returned to her apartment, Cathy felt dirty and used. Susan almost convinced her to go and talk to her pastor the next day, but Cathy overslept and missed the morning service. Monday at work Cathy finally spilled her feelings to Joan. Over lunch her friend knew how to soothe a troubled conscience.

"Do you think you're the only girl in the office who has lost her virginity! Don't worry about it. You just grew up a little."

Joan was right. Some of her friends in the office did enjoy this pleasure from time to time. There was some concern about AIDS, but if precautions were taken, most believed there was little danger. Their lives didn't fall apart because of a little illicit sex.

Cathy was offered her first joint during her lunch break, and her first experience with cocaine came at a Saturday night pool party. She never felt so lighthearted and confident—confident enough to keep dating Mick. An invitation to spend a weekend fling with him on his yacht in Galveston was the culmination of a series of exhilarating highs.

Cathy's parents heard nothing from their daughter for three years. The police tried to trace her, but the computer readout was still zero after a few months' investigation. Cathy's name became another statistic in the runaway file, but her parents kept praying and hoping.

Life-changing choices! Like Cathy, my kids and your kids will have to make them on their own someday. Our parental responsibility is to prepare them for graduation day, for a safe solo flight. A monastery cannot shelter them, and the school of hard knocks (live-and-learn) could kill them. But, turning this around, the learn-and-live philosophy assumes that we know an expert on child development whom we can count on! Allow me to introduce a genuine expert. His insight into life was so sharp that some have called him the wisest man who ever lived. He can help our kids to avoid the mistakes Cathy made.

The Benjamin Franklin of Ancient Israel

Who comes to mind when I mention the words *proverb* and *Poor Richard's Almanac?* For the American it is Benjamin Franklin. In ancient Israel the name that epitomized proverbial teaching was not Benjamin, but Solomon. God entitled His handbook for skillful parenting "The Proverbs of Solomon, the Son of David, the King of Israel" (Proverbs 1:1).

Talk about a man with experience! Solomon possessed greater political power than a United States president, more wealth than Texas billionaire Ross Perot, and more women than *Playboy's* Hugh Hefner. He spent most of his life experimenting with power, wealth, and sex in an attempt to discover what would yield lasting satisfaction. He learned reality the hard way—by experience. So why is he the principal human author of Proverbs? Because he tried it all. He was an "A" student in the school of experience. He knew the facts of life firsthand. Therefore, if our children will listen to his instruction, they can learn from his example and avoid going to the school of hard knocks themselves.

In pithy, easy-to-remember maxims Solomon encapsulated the principles of skillful living he gleaned from his own experience and from the collective experience of Israel and the surrounding Near Eastern kingdoms. He epitomized a wisdom movement in Israel that endured. Two hundred and fifty years after his death scribes in the court of Hezekiah were not only composing their own wisdom sayings (Proverbs 22:17–24:34), but also preserving the proverbs of Solomon (Proverbs 25:1). These wise men took their place along with the priest and the prophet as spiritual guides in Israel (Jeremiah 18:18). God inspired some of their advice concerning the training of the young and preserved it for us in the Old Testament book of Proverbs.

This divine instruction manual does not immediately plunge us into the difficult waters of understanding 375 solomonic proverbs (Proverbs 10:1–22:16). Instead, a brief introduction (Proverbs 1:2–6) and motto (Proverbs 1:7) state the purpose of the book and its foundational principle. Then a lengthy exhortation from a wise dad and mom seeks to incite us to pay attention to what Solomon and the other wise men have to say (Proverbs 1:8–9:18).

These parents adopt a practical motivational technique. "Listen to what we tell you, and life will reward you. Reject our instructions, and you might not live to tell about it."

We cannot expect our children to eagerly accept this "preaching." They need to see wisdom fleshed out in our personal lives. We must not be like the parent who delivers a lecture on the risk of lung cancer while shaking another cigarette out of the box and asking for a light.

All of us know that what we are speaks so loudly our children are deaf to what we say. Solomon's life reiterated this truism. He had the right ideas in his head but not in his life. Rehoboam, Solomon's son (1 Kings 12), followed his dad's life, not his words. Rehoboam's foolish pride was deaf to good advice. He demolished the united kingdom his father and grandfather had given their lives to create (1 Kings 12:16–17).

Our children will also rebel against hypocrisy. They need to see a consistent life, not just right words. The purpose of Proverbs is to reveal how to do this—how to internalize skillful living in our personal and family life.

A Goal for Parents and Children

Effective parenting is more than teaching facts about life or the Bible. Our kids might be champion Bible trivia players, but this does not guarantee they will have moral character. The memorization of biblical facts and verses is a beginning, but we must go on to ask what God is teaching about Himself, ourselves, and life. Our daily walk must illustrate how to apply biblical principles in the changing circumstances of real situations. If our children see genuine satisfaction in our lives resulting from the application of wisdom, they will desire to follow our example. The introduction to Proverbs states the moral for parents and children this way: "to know the art of skillful living which comes through disciplined training; to discern the words of insight" (Proverbs 1:2).

To internalize this purpose we must discern the meaning of three words—knowledge, wisdom, and discipline.

Knowledge

When the Hebrews spoke about *knowledge*, they had in mind far more than filling in the right box on a multiple choice exam or getting a 1600 on the SAT. A cassette recorder can out-perform humans at rote memory tests every time. True education begins with memorization, but goes on to include the application of this information in changing situations. A student may score high on a sex information exam in school, but can he resist the seduction of an immoral person who is attempting to seduce him?

We need to think through these life situations with our children. They need us to explain the whys, not just give commands. The goal is more than obedience. They must learn to see past initial choices to their consequences and then commit themselves to behavior that will produce lasting satisfaction. In the school of wisdom the student does not pass until he knows how to respond in real-life situations. Practical values need to be knit into the fabric of their lives.

Wisdom

When the sage spoke of *wisdom*, he did not mean some ivory-tower, impractical ideal unrelated to life. To know wisdom meant to internalize moral and spiritual values deep within your personality, so you could skillfully apply them in concrete situations. The Hebrew term for *wisdom* was so practical it was often used to refer to the skill possessed by an expert craftsman or sailor.

When I was a teenager, my dad and mom took me on vacation to Nassau in the Caribbean. A small sailboat was tied to the pier, and the ocean challenged me to demonstrate my prowess as a seaman, which I had learned on the treacherous lakes of upstate New York. I convinced my dad to go along.

After tipping the craft over three times and almost drowning my father, it became obvious I was not prepared to sail in four-foot surf. I was not yet a wise sailor. To make it in that bay, I needed more than book knowledge about the parts of a sailboat. I needed specific, applied knowledge about sails, wind, currents, and the proper handling of a small craft in such difficult seas. The owner of the boat possessed this skill, and I enjoyed several safe sails with him.

Wisdom in Proverbs is the ability to sail safely through the difficult seas of life. The only way to obtain this skill is through disciplined training and practice under the tutelage of a mature teacher.

Discipline

If one is studying a trade, a sport, or music, we automatically assume that training and disciplined practice are necessary to become skillful. For example, my older brother is an expert piano player, but he did not acquire this expertise by sitting down at the piano at the age of seven and deciding that he would play Chopin's *Ballade* in G Minor, op. 23. He took lessons from one of the most gifted piano teachers in the U.S. While I was out playing with the football, he was inside practicing his scales and the progressively harder pieces with which his piano teacher challenged him. Today he can play with skill and freedom. I cannot. The difference? Skillful teaching and disciplined application.

In the moral matters of life we naively believe things will work out by themselves, yet we do not make such an assumption for something as relatively simple as playing a musical instrument or sailing a boat. Proverbs counters this laissez-faire parental attitude by stating that wisdom's goal is to help the teenager "to internalize the art of skillful living, which comes through disciplined training; to discern the words of insight; to acquire the discipline to act with foresight and reason, doing what is right, just, and fair" (Proverbs 1:2–3).

What standards should we live by? How do we apply those standards in everyday situations? How do we apply those principles fairly? The answers to these difficult questions do not come by chance. They come to those who receptively listen to the instruction of wise teachers who believe in God's standards. And they come to those who discipline themselves to learn how to make distinctions between choices that will result in good and those that yield disaster. The goal of Proverbs is for parents and their children to learn to internalize the ability to live a skillful life. This skill can be gained only through discipline.

The introduction concludes with a promise to any teenager who responds to the instruction: he or she will become the proud owner of a wise head on young shoulders.

The Naive Novice

To give shrewdness to the naive, to give to the young the ability to formulate successful life plans. (Proverbs 1:4)

No teenager wants to be called a naive novice! So why does God use this label to refer to one of the principal groups He wants to reach?

The dictionary defines *novice* as an individual who has no previous training or experience in a specific field or activity. For example, a novice in snow skiing decked out in designer skiwear seeks to accomplish the seemingly impossible feat of making it over to the beginner slope. With teaching, this beginner will learn the art of the snow plow. Add a little disciplined commitment, and the advanced techniques of the parallel and stem will not be out of reach. The novice has the potential to become an expert and to experience the exhilaration and freedom of skiing down a treacherous, advanced slope in full control.

However, if this novice is a "know-it-all" who pridefully rejects expert help, choosing rather to learn in the school of hard knocks, he will probably end up with a broken leg, a ski pole through his calf, or his head buried in an eight-foot snowbank after a wicked fall. Obviously, the purpose of Proverbs is not to teach skiing, but it is to teach an inexperienced beginner how to skillfully get down the treacherous slope of life like an expert.

God is not being critical when He refers to teenagers as naive novices. By definition, the young have not lived long enough to acquire the knowledge and discipline necessary to be experts in the art of living. The crucial issue is whether they will remain naive or be willing to receive instruction.

Leafing through the proverbial pages, we develop a composite snapshot of a beginning student in the school of wisdom. Gullibility, a cocky openness to all kinds of enticing persuasion, is the main characteristic of this student (14:15). Assertive independence causes such youths to believe they are experienced men and women in a world far advanced from the limited horizons of their parents. This naiveté makes them easy prey for the get-rich-quick schemes of a con artist or a criminal (1:10, 16:29), or for the seduction of a foxy huntress (7:7–10, 9:16–17). They are especially vulnerable when the naive teenager's mom and dad buy into this illusion of sophistication and experienced judgment. With carefree abandon, this teenager clings to his open-minded lifestyle (1:22). Like a five-inch sunfish playing with a worm, he is oblivious to the fatal steel hook at the heart of some of the juiciest, most attractive temptations.

The disciplined teaching of Proverbs can expose evil's lures. But if the naive teen stubbornly rejects this teacher or ignorantly refuses to take the time to listen, he can become hardened in inescapable foolish behavior (14:18). That behavior can even result in death as Proverbs 1:32 says: "The turning away of the simple will slay them, and the complacency of fools will destroy them" (NKJV). I used to believe that Proverbs exaggerated things slightly at this point, but after more than twenty years in the pastorate, I have experienced heartache at gravesites with dads and moms of teens who did not follow the life-giving principles of Proverbs.

It is not all bad news, however, for the naive novice. They are still young and still open-minded. Maybe they will be open to the call of wisdom. God keeps trying to reach their number (1:23, 33). By observing the disgrace that comes to someone who chooses to laugh at wisdom's teaching, they might learn about life's realities before it is too late (22:3). This is the successful ingredient of programs such as Scared Straight in which kids experimenting with drugs are taken into prison where they can see firsthand where their lifestyle could lead them.

There's still time for them to learn and live. Proverbs claims it can help the naive to become worldly wise yet remain innocent (1:4). Jesus taught us to be wise as serpents concerning the temptation of evil yet harmless as doves concerning the experience of it

(Matthew 10:16). The Intel®, Microsoft® generation has a good chance to live wisely, unless we parents fail to give them the right stuff.

The Naive Parent

When you are young, you cannot help but be somewhat naive. When you're old, you have no excuse. One of the things that concerns me as I counsel families is the lack of mature parents who genuinely assume the adult responsibility to train the next generation. One parent responds to the invasion of adolescence by frantically tightening down the screws of control while another prematurely removes the controls completely. Proverbs pleads with parents to open their ears, so they will become genuinely wise in their own lives. Then they can effectively motivate kids to follow their example. Let the experienced adult listen so that he can increase his effectiveness in training the young.

Let the individual who already discerns how to make right choices acquire the ability to steer others in the right direction (1:5). Wise parents always have ears tuned in to the wisdom channel.

Gary's parents were not naive. They listened to wisdom and built their home on the principles and values we are exploring in this book. They took the time to teach Gary how to skillfully sail in life.

Cathy's parents told her repeatedly that they loved her. They bragged about her physical beauty, and she never lacked spending money. Every Sunday they went to church together, but her parents were preoccupied with their careers and did not promote family time. There was little opportunity for discussion. It is hard to think through moral values together when everyone is busy. Consequently, Cathy never internalized wisdom. During her three years of silence toward her parents, they prayed for one more chance to spend time together.

One evening their front doorbell rang, and Jason, Cathy's fifteen-year-old brother, answered the door. A frail woman stood on the threshold. Her complexion was pitted, her clothes dirty, her speech slightly slurred. He did not recognize her at first, but then Jason shouted, "Dad, Mom! It's Cathy!"

Slowly, Cathy's parents gathered the pieces of her story together. Mick had baited Cathy with luxurious living. He praised her looks and assured her of his devoted worship. He had never found such meaning in a relationship with another woman, he said. He promised to empty his bank account to make her dreams come true. How could she have known that he was heavily involved in organized crime?

When Cathy had a bad crack trip that produced strong psychotic tendencies, he dumped her. Unlike many runaways, somehow she stumbled home alive. The school of experience was nearly fatal, but she had become ready to listen to advice. With skilled counseling perhaps she could gather together the pieces of her life.

Gary made choices quite different from Cathy's. Six years after their high school graduation he was again on the sidelines at a Friday night football game. This time he was there not to play football but to begin a career as an assistant coach and teacher.

Four years at the University of Texas majoring in history and physical education, followed by two years in a master's program in secondary education, prepared him for a teaching and coaching opportunity.

During the first year of his master's program, Gary attended a Christian singles fellowship in Austin. He did a poor job hiding his excitement when Matt, a friend from church, introduced him to a new girl who had come down for the weekend from Dallas to visit her parents. Her brunette hair and sparkling hazel eyes caught his attention, but it was her gentle smile that continued to demand his attention throughout the evening.

"Hi, I'm Gary!"

"I know," she replied. "I'm Susan Morgan. Matt mentioned you earlier this evening as someone I should get to know."

For the next year Gary and Susan took turns wearing a groove into Interstate 35 between Austin and Dallas as their dating intensified. After Gary's graduation on a beautiful evening in June, Susan, who was Cathy's former roommate, married the man who loved her. After honeymooning in the mountains of Colorado, they moved back to Gary's hometown in East Texas to begin his teaching and coaching responsibilities. They had skillfully maneuvered through the challenges of courtship and dating, but now the hard work of building a marriage began. Would they choose to continue in the school of wisdom?

Three teenagers, six years, many choices, and different results in life. Life-changing choices—we all make them, and we never stop making them! Cathy was unprepared, so she had to learn in the school of experience. Susan and Gary took the less painful course of following the advice of skilled teachers. Each individual will continue to face the challenge of whether or not he or she will live according to right principles.

Which path will our children take? They will decide for themselves, but our parental responsibility is to introduce them to a Life Planner they can respect and trust. One of their most important decisions will be whether they choose to believe there is a kind and good Life Architect. Is life the throw of the dice on a Las Vegas game table or the discovery of a meaningful Designer?

Think About It

1. For a few minutes think about the fundamental values of your home. In order of priority, write down the top five. Think of some concrete life situations in which you fleshed out these values for your children by your example. What are some opportunities this week to do this?

2. Why do we as parents insist on obedience but become impatient with the "why" questions from our children? What are some situations in which an explanation cannot be given? How can answering "Why?" become a valuable opportunity to coach our children in life?

3. What in-depth discussions have you had with your children concerning spiritual values? What precipitated these special times of communication? When was the last time your child talked openly about what was happening inside him or her? What led up to that discussion and caused it to occur? What could you do to encourage it more often?

4. Interview your kids with the question: What do we do when you try to open up to us that turns you off? How can we overcome this?

2

Respect the Architect

Have you ever complained about your monthly house payment? For many young married couples today meeting these payments is a challenge almost as impossible as buying the priceless Taj Mahal on credit. To beat this credit crunch Mary and I decided to try the do-it-yourself approach. We enlisted the help of a friend and then went to the bank. After obtaining the loan, we went to a local lumber yard and told them we needed the raw materials to build a house. A few days later two large tractor trailers moved slowly onto our newly purchased acre of land and unloaded a pile of two-by-fours, two-by-sixes, nails, bricks, wire, and roofing materials. Our house just waited to be assembled! Our day of creative freedom had arrived.

Not exactly sure of what we wanted in a house, Mary and I decided the best approach would be to start mixing cement, nailing boards, gluing PVC, and stringing wire. What an adventure it would be to see what would evolve! Trial and error marked the evolution of our home, but our construction slogan remained, "We do it our way!" After two years of creative learning by experience, what to our wondering eyes should appear but—a total disaster!

Of course, this account is untrue. Actually Mary and I did build our home with the help of a friend, but it was not a haphazard, do-your-own-thing affair. The friend who volunteered to help us was an expert who had built many homes already. Even though the interest rates were high, the bank would not give us their money until we presented detailed architectural blueprints of every inch of the proposed structure. Through constant use, these plans became dog-eared and soiled. Daily they guided us in the construction process. Six months after the foundation was poured, our family moved into a home of beauty and strength.

Why do we consider it foolish to try to build a house without the skill of an experienced architect and builder, but attempt to build a family, a far more complex task, without a life Architect? In fact many contemporary "wise men" tell us no personal life Architect or Builder exists. This question about who or what was "in the beginning"—time, matter, and chance, or the personal Creator God—is far more than an academic debate between evolutionists and creationists. Our answer determines the foundation of our home life.

A Life Architect?

Astronomer and Pulitzer prize-winning author Carl Sagan begins his bestseller, *Cosmos*, with these words, "The cosmos is all that is or ever was or ever will be." A committed believer in evolution and man's ability to solve life's mysteries with the scientific method, Dr. Sagan capitalizes COSMOS in his writing but speaks of whatever "gods" that might exist in small letters. His faith is in his brilliant intellect, and the "god" of his philosophy is the material universe. According to this Cornell University astronomer, there is no divine Architect. He claims we are not responsible to an eternal Father to whom we will have to give an account. Sagan does not believe in a divinely revealed blueprint for living. But can we be sure he has all the facts?

In contrast to this prideful worship of humanity and universe let me introduce you to a far more humble, ancient wise man. He was not as quick to speak authoritatively about creation events that no scientist was on the scene to observe. Agur was a man with a strange-sounding name and penetrating things to say. He admitted his inability to answer the question, Is there a supreme Holy One who established all things? Listen to his observations from Proverbs 30:2–4.

> If you ask me how to live a skillful life of lasting meaning or how to personally know the Supreme Being, I'm as stupid as an animal. There are theologians who profess to know all about the divine, based on their own mental deductions. I am not one of them. Who has ever gone to the edge of the universe and returned? What man can control the wind or the formation of clouds in the sky? Who created the entire earth? What is the name which discloses the true character of this Ultimate Being, and what is the name of His Son? Surely man can answer these questions if he is so wise.

This ancient Near Eastern wise man saw clearly man's inability to answer life's most fundamental questions: Where did I come from? Why am I here? Where am I going? The universe is too immense, nature too profound, man's mind too limited, and life's too short, so how can anyone resolve these vital ultimate questions about how everything began and whether a personal creator is responsible for it all? But does Agur throw up his hands and cynically say, "These questions pose a philosophical Rubik's Cube® nobody can solve!"?

In Proverbs 30:5 he confidently declares that the ultimate Being in the universe has chosen to reveal His answers to these questions in His errorless Word.

All of us must decide on what kind of a foundation we will build our homes. Like Carl Sagan, some trust in man and the material world. This option involves betting your life on your ability to give the right answer to the riddle of the meaning of life. But I believe it is far safer to build a home upon the premise that the Bible is able to identify our Creator and give His credentials.

The Architect's Credentials

I worked as a carpenter's helper during the summers of my first two years in seminary. If you have ever done construction work then you are well aware of the elite status on the job site that someone in this position enjoys. All the important jobs—pulling nails out of used lumber, jack-hammering down the concrete in pier holes that have been poured eight inches too high, and running to keep your union carpenter's nail pouch filled—belong to the "carpenter's helper" or more accurately his "go-for-it." No one even turned his head when I came on the job in the morning. In contrast, when my superintendent got word that the architect was coming to inspect the job everyone began to scurry. The architect deserved respect because he designed the building, and he would judge how accurately his plans were being followed.

Proverbs 3:19–20 reveals that God deserves infinitely more respect than any architect on a construction site. Why? Because He designed and built the cosmos. His basic credential as the Creator could not be stated more clearly, "The LORD by wisdom founded the earth; by understanding He established the heavens; by His knowledge the depths were broken up, and clouds drop down the dew."

These verses identify God not only as the designing Architect but also as the Contractor who created the stars and, more important, the earth, which is our physical home. Trial-and-error probability factors were not His construction principles. Rather, every detail was carried out according to the brilliant blueprint in His mind. He was not only the expert who created matter and built the universe, but He also maintains His creation. Even the rain against our windowpane falls according to God's design.

This design is personified for us in Proverbs. Observe how wisdom presents herself not only as God's blueprint for building the universe but also as a master craftsman who daily worked at His side.

The LORD conceived me at the beginning of His work
  before His deeds of old;
I was appointed from eternity,
  from the beginning, before the world existed.
When there were no oceans, I was given birth,
  when there were no springs overflowing with water;
before the mountains were sunk into place,
  before the hills, I was born,
before He made the earth or its fields
  or any of the dust of the world.
I was there when He established the heavens,
  when He traced out the horizon's circle on the face of
  the ocean,
when He established the clouds above,
  and firmly established the subterranean springs.
I was there when He set boundaries for the sea
  so that the water would not overflow His command,
and when He marked off the foundations of the earth.
  Then I was at His side—a master craftsman!
Daily I was filled with pleasure,
  always rejoicing in His presence.
I rejoiced in every detail of His earth,
  but I was especially delighted with humankind.

(8:22–31)

Have you ever wondered what happened before there was time? Verses 22–26 reveal to us some answers from the eternal Creator. So our childlike mind could begin to understand, He describes His creation of the cosmos like a human builder would describe a construction project. First He pictures Himself as an architect at a drafting table. "Wisdom" represents the skillful ideas and drawings which He comes up with for the construction of the universe.

The project begins (8:27–29). Wisdom now represents not only the project drawings but also a master craftswoman skillfully plying her trade in the creation process (8:30–31). Daily the Lord and Wisdom take great pleasure in their accomplishments, echoing the declaration of Genesis 1: "It is good." Did you notice what Wisdom's greatest joy was? In the midst of all the natural wonders, her greatest joy was the creation of humankind (8:31).

So why is this significance relevant to our discussion of how to teach our kids to live? The reason is simple: life is not like the roll of the dice on a Las Vegas game table. Just as skillfully thought out principles guided the construction of the universe, so the wise principles for right living taught in Proverbs need to guide the construction of our lives. The principles presented are not just nice ideas some old-fashioned religionist concocted for a Sunday school class. They belong to the essential nature of the created universe. No one can escape these moral realities.

Wisdom concludes her discussion of creation with a message to our teenagers.

> Now then, teens, listen receptively to me.
>> Those who obediently follow my lifestyle live happily.
> Obey my instruction and you will be wise.
>> Do not neglect me!
> Happy is the individual who listens to me,
>> who daily watches at my door and waits on my doorstep
>> so as not to miss a thing.
> For whoever finds me finds life itself,
>> and receives acceptance from the LORD.
> But the one who misses me, hates himself.
>> Everyone who hates me loves death (8:32–36).

Wisdom promises she can make our kids happy. If we discipline them to learn and to obey her principles, she promises to give them a happy meaningful life. But if they reject her, it's deadly. Her point is that as certainly as the natural universe was built according to skillful design principles, so God means for us to build our lives according to His skillful, moral principles. To try to live in rebellion against His moral plan is like trying to breathe under water like a goldfish for an hour. We were not designed to breathe water. We have the freedom to try, but after a few minutes, we will be dead. You can stand at the top of the Empire State Building and declare that you do not believe in gravity. You can sincerely believe you can fly. But once you jump, you can't prevent the splat on the pavement below. Likewise, if we try to live in defiance of the life-giving principles of wisdom, we will self-destruct. To reject Proverbs' blueprint for living is to reject reality! The reality is that Wisdom is man's best friend. If we fail to find this blueprint or hate its demands on our lives, we will only discover that we have fallen in love with disaster (8:32–36).

"OK!" you might say, "God's life plan needs to be obeyed because He is the original Designer. What's His daily schedule look like now? Is God an architect who drew up the original prints for the universe and then moved on to more important heavenly projects? Is He on the scene inspecting and evaluating what I do in His creation?" According to God's inspired resume, He is not only creation's Architect, but He is also our ultimate Judge.

Here Comes the Judge

Unlike a human judge or father who can be fooled, God sees everything. We never get away with something behind God's back. In fact, it is impossible to get behind His back. He sees all and knows all! Listen to these revelations!

"The eyes of the LORD are in every place keeping watch on both the wicked and the good" (15:3).

"Not even the mysteries of death and destruction pose any problem for God's knowledge. How much easier do you think it is for Him to know every thought in our hearts?" (15:11).

"We can always rationalize our actions but God knows our innermost motivations" (16:2, 21:2).

"The powerful beam of God's searchlight turns the darkest corners of our thoughts to broad daylight" (20:27).

A prostitute in Dallas came to us for counseling and asked me to ask God to take a break for a while. Her scheme was that while His back was turned, she could turn a $200 trick to help pay her debts and then come back and pick up with God where she left off. We pitied her failure to understand that no one can ever escape God's observation. But what about the secret things we think we get away with when nobody is looking? Few of us would so easily forget God's standards if we remembered that from God's perspective, we do everything at the fifty-yard line of a heavenly stadium with all the lights blazing and God observing all the action "up close and personal."

As Judge over His creation God not only knows everything that goes on, but as the supreme Ruler He supervises everything. Not even the wicked, who totally disregard their Creator, can escape the ultimate day of reckoning with Him. In the end, He brings everything to its appropriate conclusion (16:4). Our minds devise all kinds of plans, but actually our lives are controlled by His plans (16:9, 19:21; cf. James 4:13–17). Pridefully, we deceive ourselves into believing that we can choose our own steps through life. In fact, every event in our lives comes from God, and we can never completely figure out the reasons for every happening (20:24).

Have your kids ever cunningly come up with a plan that fooled you? No one has ever come up with a scheme that could beat God (21:30). Our minds are so limited that they cannot even predict the headlines for a single day with certainty, but God knows and supervises the events of each day (27:1).

Confronted with His supreme will, the only wise course is to bow before Him in trust.

But can He be trusted? Can we be sure He's not some gigantic, cosmic being playing a video game with human bleeps, coldly pushing the restart button when a human self-destructs? Yes, we can be sure! Proverbs teaches us that though He is the powerful Creator and Judge, He is also the perfect Father. His goal is to make us just like Himself.

Father Knows Best

Proverbs 3:11–12 exposes God's caring, fatherly discipline. "My son, do not reject the LORD's discipline. Do not resent it when He corrects you, because the LORD corrects the son He loves. Like a father He corrects the son He delights in!"

Earthly dads sometimes punish kids for unfair reasons. We fail to take the time to see the situation correctly. God never messes up in His child training. It is always for our good. He is a fatherly coach training us to reign as His heir by His side forever. Check it out in Hebrews 12:5–11. Our heavenly Creator, Judge, and Father wants us to base our lives on three foundational construction commitments to Him: reverence, trust, and intimacy. These are the commitments we and our children need to make to Him.

Foundational Construction Commitments

We had an eighty-two-year-old great-grandmother in our church family whose questions often prodded me to think carefully about the Word of God. One Wednesday night after Bible study, she came up to me and asked, "Dave, you taught us tonight the basic motto of Proverbs—'The fear of the LORD is the beginning of knowledge but hardened fools despise skillful living which comes through discipline' (1:7). Am I to teach my great-grandchildren to be afraid of God, to shiver with fright when the roar of a tornado ravages across the Texas plains?"

Nonie nailed me with the kind of question that my doctoral level seminary jargon could not satisfy. Is God saying that great-grandmothers should tell little children scary ghost stories about Himself? Does the fear of God mean that we should shiver with fright at the mention of His name? The following illustration has helped clarify my thinking concerning what Proverbs means when it speaks about the "fear of the Lord," a subject often mentioned (1:7, 8:13, 9:10, 10:27, 14:27, 15:33, 19:23, 22:4).

Suppose one night you found yourself in Harlem, New York City, at 2:00 a.m. The tenement buildings cast menacing shadows on the deserted streets. Suddenly, a gang of leather-coated hoodlums emerge from an alley. Their switchblades snap open, and you take off running for your life. Up one alley, down another! Your lungs crave air, but the clatter of the gang's weapons drives you on. Quickly, you turn down a long, narrow alley. You're just thirty feet from the end when a hulk of a man steps out of the shadows and blocks your escape. He's seven feet of rippling muscles, big enough and strong enough to play defensive end on any NFL team. You freeze in your tracks. Where can you turn now? The gang blocks your entrance, and the incredible monster blocks your way. With no place to run, you look into the eyes of the massive man blocking your path. Then his loving hand beckons you to come. Your heart beating wildly, you scurry behind the safety of his right knee. In that moment, terrified dread becomes reverential trust in your protector. The hoodlums are no match for his power, and you are safe in his care on a dark night in Harlem.

To fear the Lord is to realize that God wants to use His awe-some creative power not to destroy our lives, but to save and care for them. We are born into a dangerous world like Harlem. The norm is that no one gets off the planet alive. Satan, the father of lies and murder, stalks us in the alleys of life. Two thousand years ago Jesus Christ, the Promised Savior, stepped out of the shadows of eternity to fight for our eternal safety. Suspended on a Roman cross, He paid in full our sentence for sin. Easter morning He left a guarded tomb empty. His resurrection demonstrated that He alone has the power to give life that can never be snuffed out. Today He blocks your path and summons you to depend upon Him to give you this spiritual life that will last forever. Have you personally realized that He died for you and that His hand invites you to His protection so that awesome dread can become rever-ential trust in Jesus as your Protector?

The most famous verses in Proverbs are an invitation to humbly put all your confidence in the Lord.

> Trust in the LORD with your entire personality. Don't depend upon your own insights to make right choices in life. In every life situation be intimate with God, and He will make your paths straight. (3:5–6)

Remember the ancient wise man's questions: "Who created the entire earth? What is the name that discloses the true charac-ter of this Ultimate Being, and what is the name of His Son?" The answer is: God is the Creator, Judge, and Father. His Son's name and the name that discloses His true character is Jesus Christ. The foundational step in becoming wise is to kneel in reverence and trust before Him. When we trust in our Heavenly Father's love expressed in the sacrifice of His Son on Calvary, we can enjoy intimate closeness with Him.

I was five years old when someone explained to me that Jesus paid the penalty for my sin on the cross and wanted to live in my life to help me live a skillful life. I put my confidence in Him. Have you made this commitment? This is the first step toward wise living and wise parenting.

God wants us to put our arms at our sides and rest quietly in His hands. He wants us to stop depending on our own insights into how to live and to stop believing that human ingenuity can solve the riddles of life and death. He wants to teach us that the real purpose for living is intimacy with Him. In fact, the intimacy He desires is so warm that the term used to describe it in Proverbs 3:6 is frequently used in the Old Testament of the sexual intimacy enjoyed by a husband and wife. This ultimate intimacy can only begin to express the oneness God wants to enjoy with us. Rather than our stumbling down a dark, garbage-filled alley, God wants to guide us down a straight path that leads to the right destination (4:18–19).

God is on the job site. We need to respect the divine Architect. If we follow the plans of the proud humanist who tells his own story about the cosmos, we will ultimately be rebuked by the God we disbelieved. But if we depend upon His revelation, the divine Architect promises us eternal life. Reverence, trust, and intimacy—these provide the proverbial concrete foundation for living that will never crack.

Think About It

1. Discuss with your teenagers how they believe human beings arrived on earth. If someone believes that people are simply the product of matter and time and chance, how does that influence his views toward the uniqueness of the human personality, human love, and moral standards? Read Matthew 19:4–6. Did Jesus believe the creation account of Genesis was a fairy tale? Who does

He say created human beings? Why would the viewpoint of Jesus Christ be more dependable than that of Carl Sagan?

2. Jot down some characteristics of God's personality you have learned from this chapter. Children tend to think of God as being like their parents; what are some characteristics of your personality that accurately reflect traits in God's personality? What deviations need to be dealt with?

3. Have you personally explained to your children who Jesus is, how He died for their sins, and how He rose from the dead and is alive today? It is important that they relate to Him as a person and make their own decision about what they believe. Your beliefs will not insure their right standing before the divine Architect. Spend some time in prayer for the salvation and spiritual growth of each of your children.

3

The Demolition Crew

There is an Architect. More impressive, He's a loving, personal Father. Our parental responsibility is to work with Him as His Spirit seeks to woo our children toward a relationship of reverence, trust, and intimacy with Himself. Proverbs sketches out His blueprint for a skillfully constructed life. Our children are born in naiveté about this life plan, gullible to believe all kinds of false information, vulnerable to evil's seduction. Our prayers can help them to open their ears to wisdom's voice.

In Chapter 2 we met Lady Wisdom, the master craftsman over all creation. She personifies not only the facts of nature but also the facts of life—moral norms intrinsic to God's created order. Wisdom loves mankind. Human beings, the masterpiece of God's creative genius, are her pride and joy.

As we turn to Proverbs 2, we find Lady Wisdom out on the streets of our contemporary lives, no longer in the idyllic surroundings of Eden. She is a street preacher, aggressively calling to our children, warning against the peril of rejecting her call. How can our kids hear her voice? How can they be protected from joining the deadly laughter of the scoffer, the complacency of the moral dullard, or the hardness of the impenetrable block—three demolition experts intent on swinging a wrecking ball against their young lives? We need to make our public and private message consistent if we want our kids to heed her voice.

Wisdom's Public Address

Wisdom preaches enthusiastically in the street;
  she raises her voice in the public squares;

she proclaims at the head of the bustling thoroughfares;
   she presents her message in the large gathering areas
      by the city gates.

(1:20–21)

The Proverbial principles need to be heard in the privacy of our homes. But our kids must also see that our values are worth standing up for in public in the teeth of ridicule. The wisdom teachers of ancient Israel never contented themselves with only communicating their insights privately to their own families. They aggressively interacted in the marketplaces, the city halls, and the educational centers of their society. Instead of bolting up their insights behind safe monastery walls, they declared them in the public arena.

The ultimate wisdom teacher reflected this same strategy—take the message to the people. Jesus' voice could be heard in the synagogue, the religious environment of His day, but He also sat down to teach in homes, by a lake, and on the hillsides. He walked among fishermen, tax-collectors, prostitutes, housewives, and soldiers—zealously challenging them to submit to the wisdom and authority of His Father. Our kids need to see us mimicking His method as we take the Father's message into our Monday morning world. The parents of Proverbs were not intimidated by the criticism, "Spiritual values are an individual private affair. They should not be soiled in the public debates of the marketplace."

As a young boy I relished traveling with my dad into New York City to the radio stations. He loved live talk shows where his personal commitment to Jesus Christ would be publicly challenged. With my hand clasped tightly in his, we maneuvered through the crowded streets. Proudly I carried, sometimes dragged, his heavy, tan briefcase. I remember walking through the revolving door of a major network one evening. No cordial greeting or handshake welcomed us. Ten seconds before air time the host simply nodded through his cigarette smoke toward the red "On the Air" light. The engineer's hand gave the signal and the program began.

"Jack Wyrtzen, what's so special about JC? You have the audacity to go around this country trying to compel people to believe in Jesus Christ for their eternal destiny? Who does JC think He is?!"

Dad did not shrink before the ridicule. Like the apostle Paul in Acts, he responded to pressure with his testimony. "For eighteen years I treated the name of Jesus lightly, just as you do. *Jesus Christ* was an expletive to be shouted when life got exasperating. Then during a week of Army Reserve training a buddy began to explain to me the Carpenter's true identity and the gift of forgiveness He wrapped up for me on the cross. One night through the Scriptures I finally understood—Jesus was the Son of God. He loved me enough to cancel my unpayable debt of sin."

I heard Dad proclaim the gospel to agnostic radio hosts, atheists, and so-called sex experts. He preached not only to crowds in Madison Square Garden but also to the attendant taking quarters on the Garden State Parkway. Many of those attendants knew him by name and had to ask for a different tract than the one he was offering a second time.

My dad, who prayed with my brother and me before turning out the light in our bedroom at the close of a day, was not ashamed to proclaim his faith on the city streets. This combination of private integrity and public courage strongly shaped my personal commitment to the wisdom of God. I must pass this heritage of public testimony on to my children. You must pass it on to yours.

What kind of response should we expect when we go public for wisdom in the marketplace? In Proverbs, wisdom faces three demolition experts—the scoffer, the moral dullard, and the impenetrable block. They laughed at her appeal. These three fools, so dumb they mock the Architect's blueprint, seek to swing a wrecking ball against our vulnerable children. Before our kids meet them in a university classroom, sales office, or prison, we need to hand our kids a personal profile of these three destroyers.

The Scoffer

How long will you naive ones love your naiveté, and scoffers be turned on by your scoffing, and moral dullards detest knowledge?

(1:22)

Kyle is a freshman at the state university. It's the first day of class, and his schedule card reads "Introduction to Religion." Already he feels buried under term papers, reading assignments, and lab hours from his previous classes. A class in religion looked like an excellent way to get in an interesting elective in the humanities. The bell brings his 135 fellow classmates to silence, and Dr. Carson, Ivy League Ph.D. with the preppie look to match, begins his introduction.

"Students, I welcome you to class 401. My responsibility is to give you an education, specifically in the field of religion. Religion—it's the history of humanity's greatest insights but also of some of man's most opinionated stupidities. Canonical authority, the belief that the Supreme Being has spoken clearly in one religious tradition or sacred writing, is one of these brainless absurdities. Did anyone happen to bring the 'Holy Bible' with them to class?"

Sally, an eighteen-year-old from a rural Southern community, digs into her purse and hands a pocket New Testament to the professor.

"Thousands of Americans have taken this book to be the breath of God. They affirm God speaks to them in its pages. Before this semester is over I trust that no one will defend this Sunday school naiveté."

With a dramatic flourish he throws the Bible back to Sally and scoffed, "Holy Bible! It's no different than any other great literary classic!"

Many professors would be horrified at this radical display of nonobjectivity. Though the majority might not accept that God authored every word of Scripture, those who are genuinely well-read in the field would know of powerful, credible defenses of the inspiration of the Bible. As a college freshmen, Kyle might not yet have access to these theological sources which would put Dr. Carson's outburst into perspective. He will probably never discover that his professor was raised in traditional Christianity and that much of his hostility reflects the continuance of adolescent rebellion against his parents. Kyle may be ignorant of the academic defenses of inspiration or the psychological struggles his professor has against his upbringing. He should know, however, the telltale signs of the mocker, for Proverbs strongly warns against this spirit of arrogant "free thinking."

I remember that in my teens a finely tuned skill to mock others and be sarcastic won loud applause from the peer group. Most of us remember this loud, defiant struggle to understand ourselves. But a belly laugh in response to a cunning association of ideas in a Far Side cartoon is one thing. Laughing at God's advice in the Bible is quite another.

The naive youth who begins to pal around with the group that mocks sacred values begins a precarious slide toward disaster. Proverbs x-rays the personality of Dr. Carson the scoffer. Skillful parents hand their kids a dossier on this wise guy before sending them out into the world. "Insolent! Arrogant! His name is 'The Scoffer'! He behaves with excessive self-conceit" (21:24).

Prideful self-sufficiency is at the scoffer's core. Defiant cynicism makes a joke of parents who give guidelines to kids (13:1). His rejection of parental authority leads to a belligerent mocking of school officials, the police, and eventually all forms of legitimate authority (15:12). Scoffers march for anarchy. Their placards call for the overthrow of all order and structure in society (29:8). Whether it is the bloodthirsty mob of Robespierre or the bombs of Oklahoma terrorists, scoffers are expert demolition artists but impotent builders of a peaceful, orderly society. They never question whether they can build a better replacement for the structures they blow up. Their cries of ridicule deafen their internal ability to listen to wisdom's voice (14:6).

This disdain for spiritual, parental, and governmental authority should never be honored with million-dollar contracts and classed as comedy par excellence. The scoffer should not be honored as the clever professor whose intellectualism places him beyond the influence of traditional morality. Instead, the mocking spirit should be publicly disgraced. Perhaps an open punishment will warn potential mockers against this self-destructive lifestyle (19:25, 21:11). The scoffer gathers around himself an admiring gang for a time, but rejection comes in the end (24:9). He cannot sustain unity. His cunning mouth instigates constant bickering and fist-fights. Only exile from society will supplant his subversive plots and bring peace (22:10, 29:8). The Creator always has the last laugh (1:26, 3:34). When you mock the Designer, you end up suffering the cost alone (9:12).

There is hope, however, for this sarcastic master of double entendre. Wisdom calls out loudly to him. The expenditure of so much energy in making a joke out of wisdom is a telltale sign—down deep inside he still cares about spiritual values. No one invests so much in resisting something that has lost all pull on his life.

But Scoffer must open his ears. Wisdom will not call forever. Tragically, the majority of this class of fools will respond to verbal correction with hatred, insult, and abuse (9:7, 8; cf. Matthew 7:6). Sometimes the school of hard knocks softens their obstinacy. More often, they harden and never seek wise counsel (15:12). Their parents, like the father of the prodigal, must allow them to leave so they may face the full force of their incorrigibility. A few look up from the pig slop and remember their dad's fairness and love.

The second member of the demolition crew, the moral dullard, has even less time left to respond, for he has slipped farther down toward the abyss of a ruined life. Proverbs says a great deal about this fool.

The Moral Dullard

Moral dullards hate knowledge. (1:22b)

He who trusts in himself is a fool. (28:26a)

The fool is rash and self-assured. (14:16)

Their complacency will destroy them. (1:32b)

Here is the brutish materialist who complacently lives life for himself, with no regard for moral values. He is hardly dull intellectually, but his opinionated, incorrigible nature causes his brain cells to refuse to fire when it comes to the application of ethics in daily life. He is loud and flamboyant. His smug self-confidence could attract our sons and daughters if they meet him in the business world. They need to discern he is living in the eye of a hurricane. Since his companions share the pain of his destructive lifestyle when the storms of life blow (1:27, 13:20, 28:26), our children need to be trained to see past his veneer at their first exposure.

His Plastic Coating

First impressions of Mr. Dullard are deceiving. The feistiness of the scoffer is gone. This fool is self-assured (1:22), quick with his tongue (12:23, 29:20), and sometimes flaunts luxurious wealth (19:10). He is able to bring loud laughter with his coarse jokes at the bar after work (10:23). When he is prosperous and his illegalities are camouflaged, society often grants him honors (26:8). But his high-flying balloon is filled with explosive hot air. Most of the time this Archie Bunker prototype rolls through life like an untended canister of nitroglycerin. He is dangerous (17:12)! His life is full, but empty.

His Hollow Core

Deception and self-deception—they are his life. Unlike the wise man who loves God's blueprint for living, the dullard detests His life plan (1:22). Rather than trusting in the Lord with all of his heart, a major foundational specification for building a wise life (3:6), he depends upon his inconsiderate, defiant impulses (28:26).

In school, trivia rivets his attention (17:24) whereas his ears are deaf to words that humanize life with beauty, grace, and truth (14:33, 15:7, 23:9). He views the cost of tuition in the University of Wisdom as a bad investment. His heart lacks the motivation to learn right standards (14:33, 15:7, 17:16).

Inexperienced instructors will be sucked into a mire of senseless interaction if they try to deal with him on his own terms (26:4). An experienced teacher will know when to ignore him and when the situation demands a strong exposure of his prideful myopia (26:5).

Sometimes it appears that he has grasped an important life principle. But though he might memorize the words of a proverb, it remains as useless to him as the impotent legs of a cripple because he lacks the discretion to know how and when to apply the principle (26:7, 9). Like a horse or mule he understands the language of the whip but cannot be controlled by words of reason (26:3).

When he goes out into the business world, dishonesty is his technique for climbing to the top (14:8, 19:1). He wounds anyone who hires him (26:10). He cheats anyone who buys from him. His heavy thumb on the scale escalates the cost of his produce (11:1, 20:23). He misrepresents those who count on him in delicate negotiations and sells his clients out to attain his own selfish ends (26:6).

If he succeeds, he might be given positions of honor and respect (26:1, 8), but eventually his shallowness will be exposed to all (13:16). His frivolous use of wealth will make him look ridiculous and coarse. He does not develop the maturity and character that enable an individual to use material things graciously for the benefit of others (19:10). Money slides through his fingers. He consumes but does not save (21:20).

In the law courts he victimizes the innocent. On the witness stand perjury means nothing to him (12:17, 14:25). Like the scoundrels who executed Jezebel's wicked plot against Naboth and put the possession of a vineyard above the value of a man's life (1 Kings 21), this fool's mind is filled with strategies to destroy others (12:20). Doing evil is his entertainment (10:23, 13:19).

Friendly words mask his evil intent, for hatred lurks in his soul (26:23–26). Since he feeds on mental junk food (15:14), his mouth gushes foolishness (15:2, 7). He never knows when to keep quiet (12:23, 13:16), speaks hastily without thinking (29:20), and explodes in anger, igniting conflict (14:16, 18:6, 7; 29:11).

Seven character traits—pride, deceit, cruelty, malicious cunning, impetuous recklessness, perjury, and contentiousness—summarize his core. These are the abominable seven that turn God's stomach (6:16–19). This individual can count on an inheritance from the Lord—shame (3:35).

The child who grows to become this fool will despise his mother (15:20) and exasperate his father (17:21, 25; 19:13). He ruins his parents (19:13). Before this becomes our own fate and before our naive kids begin to slide toward this pain and destruction, we must warn them. Anyone who associates with this kind of individual will come to ruin (13:20, 14:7). He is as dangerous as a she-bear robbed of her cubs (17:12).

As for the dullard, there is still hope for this fool. Wisdom still offers her invitation (1:22, 8:5). Sometimes, when their foolishness yields disgrace and punishment, dullards humble themselves and become receptive to wisdom's voice (18:12). The spiritual conversion of some prominent conspirators in the Watergate affair demonstrates this hope for the arrogant secularist. Like scoffers, however, most dullards continue their slide downward (14:24).

The Impenetrable Block

This fool develops when scoffer's arrogance and dullard's moral complacency harden into impenetrable foolishness. He is completely convinced that he is right and everyone else is wrong (12:15, contrast 3:7). He never listens (18:13). His mouth explodes in anger at the slightest provocation (10:14, 12:16, 20:3). His outbursts constantly burden others (27:3) and continue into the courtroom as he rants and raves against his opponents in frequent lawsuits (29:9). Actually, everyone sees through his pompous charade. He's only a lightweight in the halls of government (24:7).

This blockhead is not retarded. He is capable of intense mental activity but uses his mind to plot evil (24:8–9). This deviousness self-destructs his own home (11:29, 14:1) and brings him under the discipline of the state (16:22). Though calamitous circumstances pound him like a pestle grinding grain in a mortar, he will not turn away from his criminal activities, for foolishness has become his essence (27:22).

He curses God for his bad fate (19:3). He mocks the ideas of repentance and confession of sin (14:9). He detests the mottoes of Proverbs, such as the statement that a reverential relationship with God is the beginning of a skillful life (1:7). He abhors God's wisdom and instruction. Often he goes to a premature grave still cursing his Creator (10:8, 10, 21).

While our children are still young and before they begin to slide toward mockery, moral dullness, and impenetrable hardness, we need to give them the facts concerning the outcome of these life pathways. Most of this training needs to be done before they hit the storms of adolescence. When our children exhibit the incorrigible, rebellious character traits of the fools and refuse to listen to our verbal instruction corporal discipline is required (13:24, 22:15, 23:13–14, 29:15).

This "rod of correction," however, must never be in the hands of rash anger. When this occurs, the parent becomes the deadly, dangerous fool. Proverbs should never be used to justify child abuse. Only the mature parent who knows that a positive word of instruction accomplishes far more than harsh put-downs will have the discernment to know when sarcastic mockery of parental authority or complacent indifference to right and wrong demand a spanking given in love. Only the wise parent can detect the lie in the modern, naive notion that a child left to himself will turn out okay. The seed of impenetrability lies in the fertile soil of all our hearts, including our children's, and we must challenge them to invite wisdom inside before their spirit hardens into concrete (14:18). We must dare to discipline.

Wisdom's Promise

If only you would have turned in response to my correction, I would have poured out my spirit on you; I would have made my words known to you.

(1:23)

Raising Worldly-Wise But Innocent Kids

52

The destiny of our kids depends upon the response of their hearts to this call of wisdom. She asks no one to clean up his internal house before she will come and take up residence in his personality. She simply asks us to stop denying our foolishness and recognize that we are heading down the wrong road. When we turn to her and humbly respond, we receive the gift of a new inner capacity to understand and apply God's design for living. The spirit of wisdom pours herself into our souls.

The New Testament presents a similar invitation. Jesus came to earth on a rescue mission. In every detail He lived His Father's blueprint for skillful living. Like Lady Wisdom He went out into the marketplaces and sent out His invitation, "If anyone thirsts, let him come to me and drink. The one who believes in me, just as the Scripture has said, out of his innermost being will flow rivers of living water." The apostle John goes on to explain what Jesus was referring to. "By this He spoke concerning the Spirit, who those who believed in Him would receive" (John 7:37–39).

Since the Day of Pentecost, the third person of the Trinity has gone out into the world to draw children into God's family. When they believe in Jesus Christ, they receive more than wise counsel about life. God Himself takes up residence in their personalities to guide them into all truth (John 16:13). My greatest concern as a dad is for each of our children to open his life to Jesus and put all of his confidence for eternal life in Him. This moment of belief causes them to receive the Holy Spirit, who alone can enable them to fulfill God's blueprint for their lives. In Old Testament times a failure to heed the voice of wisdom could lead to a premature death. Today the failure to heed the Spirit's voice as He calls us to the Savior will lead to the forfeiture of eternal life in God's presence (John 3:36).

As Mary and I have sought to make Jesus Christ the center of our home life, we have seen the Holy Spirit touch each of our children, convicting them of their sin and their need to accept Christ's gift of forgiveness. As parents we must be sensitive to these special moments when the Spirit desires to work.

One night, all Mary wanted to do after a hectic day was to remain in the prone position, nestled in the soft, living room recliner. Our older boys were already deeply engrossed in an exciting video. Jenae, our youngest, was awake, but in bed, and Joshua walked reluctantly toward his room.

"Mommy, we haven't read our Bible story yet!" Joshua prodded.

Another delay tactic. *It's already late for a school night. Why not let it go this one night?* Mary's thought pattern defended her need to stay in the relaxed position. But Josh persisted.

Wearily, Mary got up, went to Josh's room, and sat down between Josh and Jenae, who, of course, had joined the duo when she learned her brother would have a story. They found the place in their Bible storybook and began to read. Jenae interrupted, "Mommy, what is heaven like?"

Mary's answer led to a discussion about how someone could know he or she was going to heaven. This bedtime moment became the time when Jenae accepted Christ's gift of forgiveness.

Our greatest joy as parents is to know that all four of our kids have made this decision. It does not ensure they will always make wise choices. It does guarantee they possess an eternal relationship with God and have made the initial step on the path toward wisdom.

All of our children, however, must be warned concerning the consequences of ignoring the quiet voice of the Spirit's instruction. The consequences for rejecting the instructions that Dad and Mom are teaching from the Scriptures can bring a harvest of despair and premature death. In life a moment can come when it is too late to live wisely.

Wisdom's Last Laugh

Since when I called, you rejected,
  when I stretched out my hand,
  no one paid attention,
since you neglected all my counsel,
  and would not yield to my rebuke,
I, in turn, will laugh at your distress;
  I will do the mocking when your horror comes,
when it overwhelms you like a deadly storm,
  when distress hits like a tornado,
when pressure and tightening straits overwhelm you.

(1:24–27)

God allows fools to insult Him and to mock His instructions. His name is cursed, and His Word becomes a comedy routine. We all know men and women who flagrantly break God's principles and appear to be living the life of ease and comfort. The invitation to make wise decisions, however, is not open forever.

As we trace the character development of the fools in Proverbs from naiveté to mockery to complacency, a point comes when foolishness becomes incurable. Proverbs cries out that God will have the last laugh. This is not the cruel laugh of a vindictive, maligned master who heartlessly seeks to get even. He laughs at the tragic comedy, the pitiful absurdity of those who think they can rebel against their Creator (cf. Psalm 2:4). Like those who gorge themselves with green apples, the ones who reject God's counsel will vomit from their own stupidity (1:31). God cannot be mocked forever. We reap what we sow (Galatians 6:7). Proverbs does not teach "no fault/no consequence" living. Loving parents tell their kids the truth.

Guard against infiltration from a fool's character traits. Bad choices can lead to irremediable consequences. Yet only God, we must remember, decides when the moral dullard becomes the impenetrable block. I am thankful that regarding eternal destiny our Creator abounds in grace.

Three more days and this rough draft of my dissertation has to be on the registrar's desk. I was just settling down to the frustration of distilling three years of research on the prophet Hosea into something that would express the thoughts God had been teaching me when the telephone rang.

"Hi! Haven't been in touch for a while! I have a friend with me who needs to talk with you. Can we come over?" The voice in the receiver belonged to Charisse, a girl in Dallas with whom our church family had been working for the past three years. We had invested hours sharing biblical principles with her and seeking to meet her needs. Yet her life continued to be a spiritual roller coaster of prostitution and drugs, apparent repentance, growth in Christ—and then the return to her cesspool. As I waited for the two girls to arrive, I argued with the Lord about bringing another person like this into our lives, especially with my rough draft unfinished on the desk. The Spirit's voice reprimanded me, "Dave, I alone decide when someone is impenetrable. I care a lot more about people than I do about academic papers."

The two girls arrived, sat down in the study, and lit up cigarettes. The new girl was frail and tired. She introduced herself as Gayle, and with encouragement from her friend, she launched into her story. It was tragically familiar.

Rebelling against her parents, she started taking drugs as a teenager. Light drugs led to heavier ones until she had a desperate need for a daily fix of heroin. Heroin was expensive, and her beautiful teenage body could bring a good price on the streets of Dallas, so Gayle became a prostitute. Scoring and fixing became her way of life until a dirty hypodermic needle caused her to contract an infection that severely damaged the aortic valve of her heart.

After surgery, the doctors warned her. Another infection would be deadly. But Gayle returned to her peer group and immorality, and the abuse of her body continued. When Gayle's enslavement to drugs had destroyed her reliability as a mother, her older sister was forced to take custody of Gayle's daughter. Concluding her story, her eyes welled up with tears as she showed me the wallet-sized pictures of her little girl. She slumped in her chair and sighed, "I guess I'm hopeless!"

The Bible on my desk was open to Hosea 2. I had been working on verses 2–23 where God used the symbol of a wife who became a prostitute to represent the character and actions of His people who had enslaved themselves to idolatry and sexual immorality. Gayle was amazed—God had firsthand experience with her kind of problem.

We talked about how God punished His unfaithful wife, first by removing her material prosperity (2:9), then by stopping her joyous celebrations (2:11), and finally by taking her into captivity by Assyria (11:5). Gayle began to identify. The punishment for her sin was an empty purse, hollow laughter, and enslavement to a lethal habit. Her hopeless eyes made me appreciate that Hosea did not end with God the judge forever rejecting His prostitute wife.

Gayle and I read on. We listened to God tenderly speaking to His estranged wife and proposing a new intimacy with her (2:14, 19–20). Israel deserved to be destroyed in consequence of her lifestyle. However, God graciously chose to love her freely and forgave her sin. Gayle and I went on to the New Testament to learn how God could justify such a merciful forgiveness. He sent His Son into the world to take on not only Israel's death sentence but the sentence standing against all of us.

Like Israel, Gayle could receive forgiveness and enter into an intimate relationship with God. Because Jesus rose from the dead to live forever, He could come into her life and set her free. He could give her the power to live a new life.

God courted Gayle's heart that morning. Through the simplicity of John 3:16, He asked her to admit she was perishing and place all her confidence in His Son. She bowed her head, confessed her rebellion, and thanked Jesus for forgiving her. At that moment a former prostitute became part of the bride of Christ.

Before Gayle left the study, I contacted a woman in our church who had an effective discipling ministry with girls like Gayle, and they set up a time to get together.

Gayle did not keep the appointment. My heart sank. Was she the "fool" who blurts out a sinner's prayer and uses believers when things get too hot? A call from her mother gave me the answer. Gayle missed the discipleship appointment because she was back in the hospital.

Her continued use of heroin after her first surgery had caused Gayle to contract the same infection that had previously damaged her heart so severely. When I visited Gayle in the hospital, the prognosis wasn't good. Surgery was out of the question. She needed blood. Together we prayed that God would meet these serious physical needs, and we thanked Him that though her physical body was diseased, Christ had given her a healthy, new spiritual life. She wanted so much to be given the opportunity to live wisely for Jesus.

The following Sunday was Easter, and after a day of celebrating the resurrection, Mary and I were relaxing with our kids when the telephone rang. God had worked a miracle different from the one we had expected. Gayle was home with her Bridegroom, never to face pain again. Her mom was calling to see if I would conduct Gayle's funeral service.

Driving to a North Dallas church for the funeral, I asked the Lord for wisdom. "Give me the sensitivity to comfort Gayle's family. Give me the courage to speak the truth in love."

Many of Gayle's street friends joined her family at the service to remember her and comfort each other. What was I to say?

Since her early teens, Gayle's lifestyle had hardly qualified her as the most exemplary Sunday school girl. She had rejected wise counsel and mocked her parents. She had run fast and hard. The natural result of her choices was physical death at the age of twenty-five.

The text God impressed on my mind was Romans 6:23. "The wages of sin is death." I pled with Gayle's friends to recognize the twistedness of their own path. Gayle's coffin silently testified that "the waywardness of the naive will slay them, the careless ease of the moral dullard will kill them" (1:32).

There comes a time in this physical life when it is too late to live wisely. But does it have to be too late to meet God?

The concluding phrase of Romans 6:23 brought a beam of sunlight into the darkness of that funeral: "But the gift of God is eternal life through Jesus Christ our Lord." I related to the mourners how Gayle had become God's daughter, His Son's bride. She was now rejoicing in Christ's presence, forever free from the consequences of her sin. The blood Gayle's friends had given to the hospital blood bank was not able to sustain Gayle's life. But the blood Jesus gave transformed a prostitute into a virgin bride, free to live in her Husband's home forever.

Think About It

1. Wisdom spread her message not only to her own family, but also to the public. What are some of the ways your children can observe your public declaration of what you believe about God, about His Son, and about His Word? What are some of the ways that we lock up God's message inside the walls of our churches? Think of some ways for your family to get out of their comfort zones and get the message across to unbelievers.

2. As believers it is easy for us to either withdraw from the public debate about spiritual values and morality or to invade and take over. Check out 1 Peter 3:15–16. What attitudes need to characterize our involvement with our society and what opposition should we expect?

3. I used a university classroom to illustrate one place where our children might encounter the "scoffer." Read over his characteristics with your family and then discuss other examples of where we might have to face this kind of individual.

4. Think of someone who has rejected biblical moral values but has achieved great material success. How does what we have learned about the "moral dullard" from Proverbs help us to handle this prosperity of the wicked? Do you ever envy this kind of person whose lifestyle seems so trouble free? How does Proverbs explain this apparent exclusion from the principle that the rejection of God's standards leads to ruin?

5. How do you as parents feel about corporal punishment? The reality of child abuse is used to reject all forms of physical punishment by many in our society who consider themselves experts. Is this a legitimate conclusion? Why or why not?

Review the characteristics of the scoffer, the moral dullard, and the impenetrable block. How can these attributes help us to know the kind of behavior that needs to be countered with a spanking?

6. Read the story of Gayle's life again with your family and then discuss how she illustrates both the justice and the merciful forgiveness of God.

4

Follow the Instructions

From building spaceships with Legos® to hooking up a new VCR, I love to follow the trial-and-error technique of assembly. While I sit cross-legged on the floor of our living room in the midst of a chaos of a thousand tiny pieces, Mary inevitably enters and utters her stock, wifely admonition, "Why don't you read the instructions?"

As every husband knows, of course, our wives are right. This business of following instructions not only keeps us from shocking ourselves in back of our televisions or breaking a vital piece on a son's Lego Launcher®; it can also protect us and our children from being smashed by the demolition crew in Chapter 3. The University of Wisdom stresses the importance of following directions. The requirements for admission into this life-transforming educational program are "Three R's": receptive ears, retentive minds, and a requesting mouth. Wise parents learn how to grab their kids' attention.

Receptive Ears

Tuning your ears to wisdom. (2:2a)

Listen, children, to your father's instruction. (4:1a)

My son, pay attention to my wisdom, open your ears to my discernment. (5:1)

When Mom has called to the kids, "Time for supper!" three times and has been ignored, she goes again to the back door and screams, "Now listen to me! Supper is on the table."

When a preacher becomes intense and wants to wake up his audience for his big idea he shouts, "Listen to me, people! Listen to me!" Jesus himself used a favorite expression, "Let him who has ears to hear, let him hear." Any teacher knows that was not empty tautology. The presence of a built-in receiver on both sides of our head does not guarantee the reception of the message. Listening with the mind in gear has become a rare commodity among students. This is tragic, for an open ear is the first fundamental in the learning process. I still remember one of my coaches in the ninth grade. He began with the basics and taught us not only how to win in football but also how to excel in academics. "When your seat warms the chair in class," he would growl, "turn up the volume in your ears. It pays to listen. Your necessary study time will be cut in half if you learn to pay attention." Though everyone agreed his advice made sense, few obeyed.

Throughout four years of college and nine years of graduate school, I observed many students sleeping through lectures all day, then studying all night to learn what they did not learn while they slept during the day. The wise student learns that it pays to be alert during lectures. The wise parent challenges his children from an early age to learn the discipline of attentiveness. Listen! It is the first fundamental in the school of wisdom.

Retentive Mind

And hide away my commandments as a treasure deep within. (2:2a)

My son, do not forget my teaching, but guard my commandments in your heart. (3:1)

Let loyalty and dependability never leave you; bind them around your neck, inscribe them upon the tablet of your heart. (3:3)

Grasp a father's instruction firmly, do not let it slip away; guard it securely, for it is your life. (4:13)

The computer threatens to make memorization obsolete in the modern home and classroom. Who needs to remember basic facts when you can have millions of bytes of information available at the push of the "Enter" key? The "new curriculum" movement in public education discouraged "rote" learning and instead stressed the importance of allowing the child to develop on his own. "Create an environment where they can discover their own truth."

The ancient Israelites rejected this naiveté. Children left to themselves without guidance would discover not truth but foolishness. They considered it unfair to ask every generation to rediscover the wheel in morals. Consequently, the older generation passed on to the younger generation the basics of a meaningful, godly life. Children were expected to memorize these fundamentals. What appears to the English reader to be a haphazard collection of proverbs with little connection between them is to the Hebrew reader a series of memory devices. The repetition of key words, the use of similar sounds, and the use of an acrostic poem (each verse of Proverbs 31:10–31 begins with successive letters of the Hebrew alphabet) help the information to stick in the student's mind. You can almost hear the Israelite parent in Proverbs exhorting her kids to memorize their Bible verses—"Hide away my commandments!" "Don't forget what I taught you!" "Inscribe these dependable principles not just on your clay tablets but on the flesh of your heart." Godly parents warned their children, "Don't let wisdom slip through your fingers."

Some modern educators are returning to this wise method of learning. Children do need to control a basic body of facts early in their education if they are going to be able to communicate within their culture. In his book, *Cultural Literacy: What Every American Needs to Know*, E. D. Hirsch, Jr., of the University of Virginia argues that a distaste for memorization denies a child's basic fascination with committing information to memory as indicated by spontaneous memorization of sports trivia and the complex rules of football, baseball, and basketball.* When education ignores the necessity of memorization at an early age, it denies the child access to the common store of information available to educated individuals at the critical period when he has the greatest ability to retain information. Hirsch concludes, "To thrive, a child needs to learn the traditions of the particular human society and culture it is born into. Like children everywhere, American children need traditional information at a very early age."

Proverbs agrees with Dr. Hirsch about the importance of memorizing traditions. But the traditions in Proverbs are far more important than the shared values of a human society. The Creator of all societies has put His stamp of approval upon the curriculum of wisdom presented in Proverbs. As a child I had the ability to commit large portions of Scripture to memory quickly. Sometimes Dad would motivate me to learn Scripture by giving me the challenge, "I'll give you five dollars for every Psalm you memorize." He eventually had to lower his price, so I wouldn't break his bank account. At summer camp, points were given for every verse we repeated to our counselor. If our team was behind, I would quickly learn a series of verses with the rest of my cabin in an attempt to make up the difference in points for our team. I am thankful for this stress upon the memorization of Scripture in my youth. Some of this mechanical repetition of words stuck with me. Tragically, much was soon lost. We need to begin to explain to our children the meaning of Scripture and not be content to have them simply repeat words.

Mechanical, word-perfect repetition of phrases is not the goal of the wise teacher. Students of Proverbs fail if they can only repeat phrases. They must also learn to "treasure" the principles because they have become full of meaning in their soul (2:2). Memorization with understanding shapes attitudes. Attitudes in turn become the basis of right action in the future. But what do you do when you can't figure out what a proverb is saying, when it sits limply in your mind devoid of meaning? This brings us to the third of the basic "Three R's" in the school of Wisdom.

The Requesting Mouth

If you urgently call out to discernment, if you raise your voice for understanding, if you seek her as if you were hunting for silver ore, just like you would hunt for buried treasure, then you will understand.

(2:3–4)

If any of you is lacking in wisdom, ask God, who gives to all generously and ungrudgingly, and it will be given you.

(James 1:5 NRSV)

What do we do when the text of Proverbs becomes only a sequence of symbols on the page? How should we respond when the material doesn't make sense? When our Bible reading goes cold, Proverbs encourages us to cry out to the Author. Although I have a doctoral degree in biblical studies and am a pastor, which requires studying the Bible, there are times when my insight into Scripture is empty and my motivation to keep digging disappears. During such silence the temptation is to rationalize: "Isn't it hypocrisy to keep reading when you don't feel like it, when you see no significance in these words?" An honest talk with the Author is the only antidote for these devotion-time blues. I confess the resistance of my heart. Instead of allowing guilt about my feelings to cause me to turn away from God, I turn toward Him in prayer. By talking directly to Him I reaffirm my belief in his objective presence in spite of my subjective feeling that He is absent. I cry out to Him to clarify what He is saying about Himself, about me, about life. After praying, I continue to maintain the discipline of consistent reading. His insights into the realities of life are only for those who are willing to dig deep for the treasure.

From riding a bike to mastering a word processor, every learning process involves times of apparent regression when you feel you are getting nowhere. Why not quit? Because quitters never experience the thrill of uncovering the gold. Proverbs compares the motivation required to become skillful in life to the diligence of the fever-pitched treasure hunter who sells everything he has and pours his life into the one goal of finding the buried treasure (2:4, 4:7). But wisdom pays even higher dividends than doubloons buried in the hull of a wrecked Spanish galleon at the bottom of the Caribbean. We must cry out to God to give us and our children this kind of hunger for the riches in His Word.

Several summers ago I had the privilege of speaking at a young adults' conference in Poland. Though the communist government was still in power, we were allowed to teach the Scriptures freely and to interact with the young people. Those believers had never had the opportunity to choose what style of Christian music they would listen to on the radio, or whether it would be Swindoll, MacArthur, or Stanley for their daily Bible lesson. There were no arguments over which translation is closer to the original. They cherished any translation. They coveted any moments God gave them to freely discuss the Bible.

One evening after I had lectured on Proverbs for more than an hour, the young people began to fire questions at me through the translator. Their questions continued until about 1:00 a.m. I'll never forget the words of one of the Polish students when he saw me begin to tire. "I know you're still recovering from jet lag and you have taught us many hours, but we don't often have this opportunity to sit down with a pastor and ask him our questions about the Bible. May I ask just one more?"

In spite of the difficulties of listening to me through a translator, these students were diligently hunting for the truth. As I went up to my room that night I prayed, "Lord, you have given me the privilege to live in a land of religious freedom. You allowed me to attend Dallas Theological Seminary where I was able to spend hours finely tuning the tools of Greek and Hebrew and theological discipline. All that training equipped me to study your Word and to expose it to others. But do I have the intense desire to know you and your truth that these students have shown tonight?"

If we are to become wise with our children, our entire being—our ears, our minds, and our mouth—must get involved in this search for wisdom. As parents we are responsible for implementing the "Three R's" in our own lives. We cannot force our children to follow these same instructions, but we can whet their appetites by showing them the benefits we have received by following God's instructions. We can remind them of the rich rewards this pursuit will bring into their lives. Wisdom is well worth the effort.

The Rewards for Following the Directions

Then you will understand the fear of the LORD,
   you will find intimate relationship with God . . .
Then you will discern God's standards,
   how to apply these standards in real life situations,
and how to do this with grace and fairness . . .
Discretion will keep watch over you,
   understanding will guard you,
to deliver you from the way of evil,
   from men whose words are perverted . . .

To deliver you from the immoral woman,
  from the adulteress with her smooth words . . .
So that you might walk in the way of good people,
  and keep to the path of those who obey God's standards.

(2:5–20)

The key to motivating our children is to find a prize they want badly enough. When Jenae and Josh were little, I could have supported the entire General Mills® corporation with the amount of Trix®, Franken Berry®, Lucky Charms®, and Cherrios® they ate. The reason for this consumption was not their love for cereal alone. In our family we had a rule—you could not rifle through the contents of an entire box of cereal in order to find the prize at the bottom. You had to eat your way there. Thus, Josh and Jenae spent each morning competing to determine who would get to the bottom first and thus get to keep the prize. Their motivational batteries were on "heavy duty" because they were convinced that the "invisible ink pen" or other plastic gadget would be a priceless treasure. I pray they will have this same intensity to win the rewards of wisdom—intimacy with God (2:5–8), an ability to apply His standards in life (2:9–11), protection from evil men and women (2:12–19), and the enjoyment of God's blessing in life (2:20–22). These rebates are not cheap plastic gimmicks. They are the durable gifts that protect us from breaking.

Intimacy with God (2:5–8)

Why should a child pay attention to the advice of Proverbs, memorize and internalize its principles, and cry out to God for insight when he or she doesn't understand (2:1–4)? Because obedience to these instructions will give him an exquisite appetite for spiritual values, and he will become hungry for intimacy with the Architect. This closeness with God is both the beginning and end of a life rich in value. He teaches skill to make the right turns, for

He is the Author of wise choices. If we stockpile His guidelines, He will give practical competency to meet challenges (2:7). He becomes a shield for us when we sincerely devote ourselves to Him (2:7); He becomes our stronghold (cf. 10:29), guarding and protecting every step (2:8). Though detested by the wicked (29:27), we will become privy to God's secret counsel (3:32). He will love to hear our prayers (15:8). Consequently, as His devoted worshippers, we can expect security and freedom from anxiety and fear.

Discernment of the Right Path (2:9–11)

The Old Testament book of Job wrestles with the agony experienced when, for no earthly reason, bad things happen to good people. Proverbs exposes the truth that good times come to those who choose to obey God's instructions. Perhaps they will not occur until we join Him in heaven, but they *will* come. We must remember Job when we are suffering, but we must not allow our trials to obscure the blessings that come to those who follow God's guidelines. The child who matures in godliness and develops the ability to make accurate decisions as he applies God's truth to life decisions will walk the good path (2:9). Unlike the moral dullard with his insatiable hunger for foolishness, this child will be attracted to and satisfied by a diet of wisdom (2:10). This correct information will permeate the inner life, where thoughts and feelings mingle to produce choices (4:23). Consequently, he or she will see through the cheap prizes offered by the demolition crew we met in Chapter 3 and will choose instead to obey God's morality. This maturity will deliver this child from the tragic consequences of unethical behavior.

Protection from Evil (2:12–19)

Those who oppose God are foolish, but they are also cruel and dangerous. God promises to rescue the individual who chooses wisdom from the claws of the criminal who willfully rejects the godly course of life for a path of violence (2:12–15, cf. 4:14–17) and from the talons of the sensualist who abuses sex for selfish gratification (2:16–19). The illicit use of money or sex can be deadly. Since skill in these areas is such a strategic part of wise living, we will devote the following chapters to exposing what Proverbs says about these areas. God's kids must stay away from the dark alleys of crime and immorality. Proverbs gives us the facts to help keep our kids safe. But giving them the right information does not guarantee they will make right choices. Our choices, and theirs as well, express what is actually going on in the core of our personality.

We can choose to walk along God's life path with its ever increasing insight into truth (4:18), or we can choose to stumble in the darkness of rebellion (4:19). The core of our personality determines the road we take (4:23). This explains God's constant plea, "Love me with all of your heart." We must challenge our children to choose this option.

Parents often come to me and say, "Our child is messed up. He got involved with the wrong crowd. How can we help him to get in with a better group of kids?" In the next chapter we are going to face the power of the peer group and learn how to help our kids to escape this suction into deadly companionship. However, the question that must first be faced is, "Why do our kids gravitate toward a certain group?"

Kids associate with those who have the same core values they do. Those who desire to love God with all their heart are drawn to others who have this same desire. Those who live for selfish pleasure and excitement will magnetically attract those of similar commitment. Unless the naive fool turns his heart wholeheartedly toward God, he will join scoffer, moral dullard, and impenetrable block and will be slain by their waywardness (1:32).

We must challenge our kids to place God at the core of their being, to trust in Him wholeheartedly (3:5), and then to guard this commitment as their most vital possession. We must not be afraid to have honest talks about the condition of their hearts or to face the truth about our own hearts. The real internal values of Dad and Mom—not just what we say but who we are—are the most powerful human forces shaping our children's commitments.

As I grew to maturity and began to realize that my parents were not gods or demons but human beings, I had to face the truth—they, too, were sinners. All parents are. My dad often buried himself in his ministry and neglected the development of a personal relationship with me. At forty I understand his temptation as I face the pressure of balancing work and family priorities. My mom sometimes talked too much about other people. Though my dad is a prominent Christian leader, neither he nor Mom was perfect. But through the years they were wholeheartedly devoted to their Savior.

I never needed to question the sincerity of their love. Their hearts daily belonged to Jesus. I believe this is the most important factor in explaining why all four of my adult brothers and sisters join Dad and Mom in their devotion to the Lord.

"Above all else, vigilantly guard your heart, for the impulses that determine one's life flow from this center" (4:23).

*E. D. Hirsch, Jr., *Cultural Literacy* (Boston: Houghton Mifflin, 1987), p. 31.

Think About It

1. I mentioned how my dad rewarded me for memorizing verses from the Bible. What are the rewards set up in your family for committing sections of God's Word to memory? This discipline of memorizing Scripture isn't just for kids. The danger of repeating

memory verses in a meaningless way is always a danger for children and adults. What are some ways we can make memorizing Scripture more meaningful for our family? (One suggestion would be to have our children rephrase memory verses in their own words.)

2. Family discussion: Will learning always be fun, like a Sesame Street game? Does a football player or basketball player ever go through difficult times to master athletic skills? Why should we keep at the task of understanding the Bible even when we don't feel like it?

3. Think of a personal illustration from your life where knowing and applying a principle from God's Word protected you. Share it with your children.

Money Blueprints

Use money skillfully to honor Him.
Remember, illicit wealth leads to death.

5

Bonnie and Clyde

How does a drug pusher ensnare a teenager? The scenario often begins like this.

"Ben, you've got to come Saturday night! The party is going to be red-hot—beer, music, and knockout, available women. A first-class Saturday night fever!"

How could Ben, a sophomore, turn down an invitation from a senior like Marshall? Marshall's beautiful MG and his girl—the envy of the high school—caught Ben's eye, but he looked down and said, "I could never get clearance from my dad to go to a bash like that!"

Marshall shrugged his shoulders. "Don't tell him about the party! I'll have my mom call your parents and invite you to spend the night at our house Saturday. Mom's working, so we'll just take off after she leaves. You've got to come! An old friend of mine will be at the party. He has a perfect way for you to finance that new pickup you want to buy! You won't have to bag groceries twenty hours a week anymore!"

Ben was certainly tired of filling brown paper sacks for grocery shoppers, and Marshall's plan worked to perfection. The sophisticated party sent Ben into orbit. From the tips of his toes to the split ends of his hair he'd never felt so high. When it was time to leave, Marshall's friend made sure Ben had a few depressants to help him come down.

Several months later Ben paid for his personal drug needs by selling some pills to his friends. His craving for harder stuff eventually meant that he didn't even balk at selling drugs to younger kids. At times he wanted to stop the trip, but by then he knew the names of the wrong people and had seen too many high-level deals. A beating after a party and a threat against his parents and kid sister ensured his loyalty to the organization.

Why not go to the police? Ben knew that some of the local cops had supplemented their low salary by accepting bribes from his people. Ben found himself securely wrapped in the multiple arms of the drug octopus.

That octopus sends forth its tentacles to ensnare our kids. One of my closest friends went through the agony of having to ask his son to leave his home because of a drug dependency. Experts debate on Nightline whether or not the U.S. should follow Holland's example and legalize drugs. But no one mentions that Amsterdam—a former center for spiritual renewal and biblical theology—has now become Europe's haven for drug dependency.

In 1988 Sterling Johnson, a special narcotics prosecutor in New York, declared sadly, "Every American better just pray each night that we don't lose the war on drugs." At a Bill Glass prison crusade I had this connection between drugs and violence powerfully taught to me by inmates in a state prison. As I spent the weekend presenting the gospel and sharing with inmates, each one stressed that they were in prison because of drugs and alcohol. School teachers cannot be expected to win this fight against drug dependency. Former U.S. Education Secretary William Bennett was right when he argued that schools cannot be expected to check effectively the demand for drugs when so many youngsters watch their parents feed their own addictions (*Time*, March 14, 1988).

Faced with this brutal assault against our country and our children, how should straight parents respond? It will not work to shake our heads and sigh, "It wasn't like this when we were in junior high and high school! Our kids face such sophisticated seductions. How can we hope to counteract the pressure?"

Did parents in biblical times face anything comparable to the drug problem? Popping pills was not the dominant temptation for young people in ancient Israel, but footloose, gold-studded bandits did entice rebellious teens to join their gangs. It was not a little kids' game but the real thing! Lifestyles like Butch Cassidy and the Sundance Kid or Bonnie and Clyde were "in."

The godly parents of Proverbs did not retreat in bewilderment. They fought back. They committed themselves to take the time necessary to teach their children the deadly realities of living for illicit highs. They began the training by saying, "My son, if criminals entice you, strongly refuse!" (1:10).

Parents Not Afraid to Say No (1:8–10)

Observe that this dad had moral guts. He didn't sit in his Lazy Boy® and hope his son would never face the undertow of the ocean of crime. He didn't lock his son in a monastery to keep him away from evil's deadly pull. Instead, he faced the facts. In the real world his son would most likely be propositioned at some point by the criminal con. In anticipation of just such an occurrence, he laid down a clear-cut response, "Don't give in!"

Parents Not Afraid to Answer "Why?"

How do your young people respond when you lay down an authoritative command? Probably with the universal teen challenge, "Why?" How do you respond when hit with this challenge? The authoritarian parent feels threatened and retorts with the basic turnoff, "Because I said so!"

The Bible does teach teenagers to respect and obey their parents (Ephesians 6:1). Rebellious attitudes are sinful at any age, including the teen years. There are situations when parents can't explain all the reasons for their decisions. But authoritative parents, in contrast to the authoritarians, view the "why" questions as moments of opportunity. These are the charged moments when they can pour street-smarts into the minds of their children.

The Criminal's Bait

Using role-play as the teaching method, the father lets his son listen to a criminal's sales pitch designed to entice a naive young person to join the gang. Check out Proverbs 1:11–14.

> Come on and join us!
> > Let's lie in wait to spill the blood of our victims!
> > We'll ambush the unsuspecting innocents!
> Just as death devours life, as certainly as those
> > in the bloom of health can suddenly fall into the
> > pit of death we'll be invincible.
> We'll secure all kinds of precious wealth.
> > We'll fill our houses with plunder.
> Throw in your lot with us,
> > and we will share a common purse.

Observe this sales talk carefully. Three juicy worms bob enticingly before the prospective catch, and our kids are the victims who could get hooked. What's the bait? *Invincibility, instant wealth,* and *intimacy.* They are still juicy bait today.

Invincibility

A perverse magnetism lies in believing that you are an invincible, high-rolling thief and murderer. Think of the movies that have made millions by portraying this swashbuckling hero who blows away anyone and everyone who gets in his or her way. It's heady to equate yourself with the relentless power of death. We all want to be winners, and the criminal's promise is "Victory—swift and easy! No one will be able to stop you!" He uses the worn-out, ancient line "We'll never get caught."

Bonnie and Clyde

Though Clyde Barrow stood just 5 feet, 5-1/2 inches tall and weighed barely 127 pounds and Bonnie Parker couldn't edge the scale past 100, with a finger on the trigger of a Browning automatic rifle Bonnie and Clyde were veritable giants. Guess who supplied the Barrow gang with guns and ammunition? On February 19, 1934, they cockily armed themselves courtesy of the U.S. government after burglarizing the National Guard Armory in Ranger, Texas. They miraculously escaped one police roadblock after another and blasted their way out of certain capture.

In the early thirties, the Barrow gang was invincible. Newsboys jumped for joy when the names Bonnie and Clyde appeared in bold print on the front page. The fame of this elusive couple sold thousands of papers. Bonnie and Clyde seemed invincible, and that invincibility is the first lure in the criminal's persuasive arsenal (1:11).

The second enticing prize is easy money.

Instant Wealth

Why work for money when you can steal it? Like soldiers rummaging through the wealth of a defeated city, the criminal promises you "easy pickin's, a quick million."

Just a week after the Barrow's gang replenished their arsenal from Uncle Sam's supply, Clyde and his partner, Ray Hamilton, knocked over the bank in Lancaster, Texas. Their women waited in a switch car just south of town. Minutes after the robbery, Ray and Clyde abandoned their original getaway car to be free of the incriminating license plate and sped off with their beauties and the biggest payday yet—$4,433. That kind of money in 1934 could put some respectable threads on anyone's back and buy a lot of pleasure in a distant city. The well-worn criminal line is always, "Who says crime doesn't pay?"

The promises of invincibility and instant wealth are powerful, but they cannot match the firepower of crime's third promise: close friendship.

Intimate Companionship

Teens feel a passion to belong to the group. When I was sixteen, I found out just how powerful group influence can be.

I was working at Word of Life Ranch, a children's camp in upstate New York. One of my friends was a first-class womanizer. He not only had a girl at the Ranch, but he also dated a girl at the teenage camp eight miles up the lake, and another at the adult camp. On his days off he would parcel out his time between the two up the lake, and during the week he was with his girl at the Ranch. The key to his success was his beautiful, blond hair, and a group of us decided to remedy the situation.

One night, while he was talking with his Ranch girl in the staff lounge, four friends grabbed him. After forcing him into a barber's chair, we took shears to his head. Have you ever seen pictures of Mohawk Indians? Then you've got the picture of our former friend's head. But the physical strength of four boys controlling one is not the real power of a group that I observed that night.

The next morning at the flag-raising ceremony twelve counselors stood behind their line of campers respectfully facing the flagpole with hats on their heads. However, you cannot keep your hat on during the raising of the American flag. When the hats came off, the flag-raising halted. Four hundred campers went into hysterics at all the Mohawk haircuts. You say, "Dave, I thought there was only one haircut that night." That's how many there was to start.

As soon as I put down the clippers that night, the group grabbed me. When my hair was all over the floor someone decided this Mohawk haircut was the "in" thing! Like the plague, one guy after another joined in. When it was over, we had a group of more than ten with weird haircuts. Now if you had asked any of those fellows individually if he wanted his head shaved, except for a strip of hair down the middle, every one would have thought you were crazy. But get the group pressure going, and any of us is capable of doing something stupid. Being influenced by the wrong group can get us to do things a lot more foolish than getting a Mohawk haircut.

The criminal knows about the persuasive power of peer pressure. His line therefore becomes an invitation to join the high-rolling set. His gang is where the action is. He seductively smiles and says, "Cast your fate to the wind! Join our free-living lifestyle! You won't have to fend for yourself. We'll all draw from a common purse. We'll be in this together" (1:14).

Perhaps you saw Hollywood's version of *Bonnie and Clyde*. It received all kinds of critical praise back in the '60s and has been aired on national TV several times since. Who wouldn't be drawn to the love affair between the handsome Warren Beatty and the stunning, youthful Faye Dunaway? While on the run, Bonnie writes beautiful poetry for her Clyde, and they make love in romantic motel settings. Sure, they rob banks, but they throw money to the poor as they escape from town.

When watching this type of movie, you find yourself admiring the bad guys. Given the opportunity, who wouldn't be tempted to join them? As you are drawn into the movie version of Bonnie and Clyde, the deputies hot on their trail subtly become the enemy, and the thieves become the heroes. But is all this for real? What is the truth about a life of crime?

The parents of Proverbs permit their children to feel the undertow of crime's appeal—invincibility, instant wealth, and intimacy. Then they expose the hard-core truth: crime is cruel, stupid, and self-destructive.

Crime's Hard-core Reality

My son, do not associate with them in their lifestyle.
   Don't even take the first step down their path of life,
because their feet run to injure their victims.
   They eagerly hurry to shed blood.
Surely it is useless to spread out a net
   to trap birds while they watch you set the trap!
But the criminal lies in wait for his own blood.
   They ambush their own lives.
Such is the destiny of everyone greedy for unjust gain.
   It takes away the life of those who get it.

(1:15–19)

Bandits on television and in the movies shoot and kill, but the bloodstained shirts can be easily cleaned. When the director yells "Cut!" the actor jumps to his feet for another scene. The real-life bandit, on the other hand, is intoxicated with the blood of his victims. The deadly reality is that he hurries to commit the next murder because of the sheer exhilaration of killing. The yell is not "Cut" from a movie director but "Oh, God!" from a young widow whose husband has just been blown into eternity.

Stringtown was a quick stopover in southeastern Oklahoma. On Friday evening the biggest thing going in town was the roadside dance. The hottest thing at the dance that night was the whirling, beautiful little blond in a flaming red dress. Dancing with her two well-dressed male companions, she was the princess of the evening. A local fellow asked the stunning stranger for a dance but was roughly pushed aside by her companions. The moonshine whiskey flowed freely. When the woman and her friends jumped into his car, the rebuffed youth went to the local lawmen for help in removing the outsiders.

Bonnie and Clyde

Sheriff C. G. Maxwell and his deputy E. C. Moore approached the vehicle expecting to investigate a routine misunderstanding. "What's going on here?" Moore asked the strangers. A volley of gunfire was the response, and Moore slumped with a bullet through his forehead. Maxwell fired but was critically wounded by the onslaught of bullets from Bonnie, Clyde, and Ray Hamilton's automatic weapons. This was just one of the cruel murders that bloodied the historical path of the real Bonnie and Clyde. A path strewn with eleven murder victims and six others critically wounded.

I pastor a church in Midlothian, Texas, a small town southwest of Dallas. Bonnie and Clyde often used Midlothian as a hideout from the Dallas lawmen. My next door neighbor was raised by his grandfather W. A. Parker, Bonnie's uncle. In my living room my neighbor shared his impressions of the real Bonnie and Clyde.

"I remember it was late in the evening at my grandfather's home seventeen miles east of Crockett, Texas. I was sitting on my grandmother's lap when a brand-new Model A Ford drove up. The adults suddenly became quiet, and I sensed their fear. Bonnie got out of the car. Clyde nervously waited outside the yard by the gate without killing his engine. Bonnie, a very small woman, approached us. Her hair was all matted. 'We need some food and some help to get down the road!'

"I can still feel the terrible fright in my grandmother as Granddad refused to help. Bonnie's eyes were cold as steel. No one breathed until they roared away.

"Granddad often described Bonnie as a little thing, but tough as nails. The kind of woman who could machine-gun you in the face and then spit in the pool of your blood without batting an eyelash."

The street-smart individual will never forget that real crime produces a cold, callused enjoyment of violence. Violence yields the horror of a mother's tears at a gravesite and children who grow up without their daddy. The irony of it all is that the ultimate victim is the "invincible" murderer himself.

You've heard the expression "You're a real bird brain!" Our kids need to learn that a criminal's common sense makes a bird's brain look like Albert Einstein's.

If you have ever done any kind of bird hunting, you are well aware of the fact that one does not stand up and shout, "Look here, birdie! Take a peek at my new twelve-gauge!" To do so would alert them to your presence and cause them to abruptly change their flight pattern, making it difficult to get a decent shot.

Ancient Israelites did not use shotguns. Nets provided the means for snaring birds, but the idea was still to not let the birds know what was going on. That's the point of Proverbs 1:17–18. Even a stupid bird knows enough not to get caught in a trap when it sees it. But the criminal is even more stupid than a bird. He flies right into his own ambush. When you live by the gun, you die by the gun.

A few months before her death Bonnie wrote these words,

> They don't think they're too tough or desperate,
> They know that the law always wins;
> They've been shot at before,
> But they do not ignore
> That death is the wages of sin.

> Some day they'll go down together;
> And they'll bury them side by side;
> To few it'll be grief—
> To the law a relief—
> But it's death for Bonnie and Clyde.

Although they knew the end would be violent death they kept running until May 1934.

Outside the Majestic Cafe in Shreveport, Louisiana, Bonnie and Clyde waited impatiently for their new young partner, Henry Methvin, to purchase a stack of sandwiches and some soft drinks. Two police officers cruised by. Bonnie and Clyde were sure they had been spotted. Leaving Methvin behind, they took off. The police commented later, "We didn't even notice them until they sped away." Proverbs 28:1 states, "The wicked flee when no one pursues."

The officers took up the chase until they recognized that the couple might be the desperate duo. The policemen, seeing they were outgunned, abandoned their pursuit and reported to their superiors. Back at the cafe Methvin abandoned the sandwiches and quickly left.

Having trailed Bonnie and Clyde for two years, Dallas deputies Bob Alcorn and Ted Hinton knew the habits of the duo better than those of their own wives. They happened to be in Shreveport when the report about the jumpy couple came in. With Methvin on foot and his father's place about fifty miles east of Shreveport, the deputies knew it was only a matter of time before Bonnie and Clyde would try to pick up their partner at Old Man Methvin's. There was only one gravel road back to his place. Just off this road, on a high point commanding a half-mile of country road in either direction, Alcorn and Hinton concealed themselves in some underbrush with four fellow officers. Their arsenal of automatic weapons could have blown an oncoming tank off the road. They waited there with the mosquitoes and snakes.

Two days later, at 4:17 a.m., they heard the familiar cough of Old Man Methvin's Model A Ford truck. The armed police halted him. "What are you doing out this early in the morning? Where's Clyde? Has your son contacted you?"

Methvin cursed and revealed nothing about Bonnie and Clyde's whereabouts. Since he persisted in maintaining silence, the officers took him several feet behind their position and handcuffed the old man to a slender tree.

Turning his truck around, they quickly took off one of the tires and jacked the vehicle up in the middle of the road. Should Clyde drive down this road the truck would force him to slow. The officers had played this game before, and this time they set the bait perfectly before settling in to their vigil. Methvin's father cussed in the background from time to time.

At 9:15 a.m. that morning Hinton heard the sound of a motor. A car sped toward them. *Full speed is the only speed Clyde knows*, Hinton thought. Having grown up in West Dallas with the notorious outlaw, Hinton recognized him instantly. "This is it! It's Clyde!" he whispered.

Clyde spotted the truck and slowed. Bob Alcorn stood. "Halt!" His shout shattered the morning calm. Bonnie screamed, Clyde grabbed for his rifle, but like a sheet of rain in a cloudburst, the shells struck his weapon, making it useless. Reaching for a pistol, he tried to get away, but the steel-jacketed bullets easily penetrated the car and ripped his flesh. Bonnie slumped over, her right hand blown off. Fifty-five shells riddled Clyde's body. The mortician later counted fifty through Bonnie. Those who had brought so much grief to others were ambushed in the same machine-gun hell they had inflicted on others.

Contrary to Bonnie's poetic prediction, the two do not lie side by side in a Dallas graveyard. In their book *Ambush: The Real Story of Bonnie and Clyde*, Ted Hinton and Larry Grove quote Mrs. Emma Parker's response to her daughter's request, "Clyde had her for two years, and look what it did for her."

Association with lawbreakers also caused death three thousand years ago when the father in Proverbs taught his teenagers.

In the thirties the career of Bonnie and Clyde illustrated the criminal's foolish self-destruction. But does Proverbs 1:10–19 still claim to have a handle on reality today?

I was gathering up my notes after lecturing on this passage at a Bible conference when a middle-aged woman came up to me. "Dave, do you have a minute?"

"Sure! I'm just trying to get these overheads put away."

She hesitated and then went on. "My husband and I were divorced. Our teenage son was living with me when he met a new friend at school. I did not like the group this friend ran with, but my negative comments were always met with 'Mom, somebody with his head screwed on right needs to be his friend!' A few times I suspected that this friend was on drugs, but my son was spending more and more time over at his house and less time at home with me."

Her eyes moistened, "One afternoon, over at his friend's house, my son was shot through the head. His friend was high on drugs."

As I weep with this mother, I ask, why this needless waste of lives? Most sports fans remember the 1986 cocaine death of basketball star Len Bias, and my hometown, Midlothian, remembers the brazen assassination of George Raffield, an undercover police officer, by two teenagers. This must cease.

Parents, we must speak with authority to our children about the seduction of drugs. "My son, do not associate with them in their lifestyle. Don't even take the first step down their path of life because their feet rush to injure their victims!" (1:15). Many of our young people are wising up to the destruction of drugs, but what about sons and daughters already ensnared?

Like the hole in the face of his beat-up guitar, Tom knew he was empty. A summer escape from the heat of New York City to the coolness of upstate Lake George was not refreshing his burned-out emotions. He had been a leader in the Hippie movement of the sixties. He had spoken of free love and had led demonstrations in Central Park. In reality, however, he was a slave now. Spaced out on drugs, he sat by the lake strumming his guitar.

"Hi, my name is Bruce. Do you mind if I sit down?"

Tom nodded to the college student, and through the fog in his mind tried to make sense of the small talk.

"I'm working up the road at a summer camp for young people named Word of Life," Bruce continued. "Why don't you come up and spend a few days. It'll be a blast. Good food, music, and sports!"

Why not! Tom thought. *I'm tired of playing in the club. A few days of free food and a place to stay before returning to the city would be all right.*

The drugs inside made the speedboat ride across to Word of Life Island seem like he was flying in the clouds. When the men in his cabin introduced themselves as Peter, John, and Paul, Tom thought he had died and gone to heaven. In the meeting that night the message was about how a person could be sure he'd end up in heaven.

Tom heard about Jesus Christ, a divine man who claimed He could give meaning to life. As the evangelist related the simple gospel, Jesus confronted Tom personally with his need for forgiveness. Jesus had died in His place. He claimed to have risen from the dead. Tom knew he had to make a decision about who or what he would depend upon. That night he received the Son and became a child of God.

He called his girl in New York City. Vicki came up to see him, and when he explained what Christ had done for him, she too opened her heart. For the rest of the summer they stayed at Word of Life and were strengthened in their relationship with Jesus.

The disciplined reading of the Scripture acted like fresh water cleansing a filthy sponge as Tom and Vicki opened their minds to

God. Though they had lived together for over a year, they broke that intimacy. Free of drugs and immorality Tom and Vicki began their college studies that fall. Did the new life last?

After completing their studies and getting married, Tom and Vicki Mahairas moved to New York City to begin a new church. Today Tom is affectionately known by the members of Manhattan Bible Church as Pastor Tom. "For the wages of sin is death but the gift of God is eternal life through Jesus Christ our Lord" (Romans 3:23).

Think About It

1. Parents, what are some areas in which you have set a strong standard of moral discipline? Some areas of weakness? How is this reflected in your children's behavior?

2. Listen to your children's conversation, especially with their friends from school and when they forget you are around. What are some of the "in" groups according to your teenagers? What kind of influences are these groups having?

3. Family discussion: Retell some of the things you have learned from Proverbs 1:8–19. Be careful not to get "preachy." Share some experiences from your own life and ask your kids to express their views on issues like drugs, nightclubbing, and immorality. Listen to them!

4. Pray together as a family, and ask God to give you wisdom and strength to resist the seduction to live for illegitimate wealth and illicit thrills. Thank Him for the pure pleasure He can give.

6

The Sting

Chet settled at his desk and opened his English textbook. His first midterm exams loomed one week away. As a freshman he wasn't sure what to expect. At least he had time in the evening to concentrate on his studies and not worry about trying to work a full-time job. All the sweat and strain of working construction for three months in the summer was paying off. He could relax about his tuition for the year. The money was safely waiting in the bank.

Better hit this grammar, he thought, trying to get the study juices going, *or I won't need money to pay for classes!*

He was in the middle of memorizing the definition of "syntax" when two neatly dressed strangers knocked at his dorm door and immediately entered.

"Hi, the name is Harry. This is my associate Wilson. Have a few minutes to talk? Fred, next door, got really excited about an opportunity we can make available and said you might be interested in it as well."

Chet glanced at his English text, then at his watch. "It'll have to be quick. Got a test on Monday and this grammar doesn't stick upstairs easily."

Harry grabbed the other chair in the room, turned it around backwards and sat facing Chet. "I promise this will take only five minutes. Five of the most valuable minutes you ever invested." With that his briefcase snapped open, and he began his pitch.

"How many students attend this university? Let's say twenty thousand. Do you know how many pens and pencils they are going to purchase this semester alone? Every single one of them will purchase

91

at least some writing utensils. Why let Bic® and Papermate® make all the money? Imagine how many of your classmates would buy from a fellow student if he offered them a special university-edition pen and pencil set like this one at a good price?"

With a flourish Harry opened the elegant box in his hand to reveal his product. Chet had to admit—the fountain pen and matching pencil with the university logo engraved on the side were first-class.

"Chet, these retail for twenty dollars a set. But the unique opportunity for you tonight is that I am prepared to give them to you wholesale for ten dollars. For an initial investment of eight hundred dollars, I'll deliver eighty pen and pencil sets right here to your room. You sell them for twenty dollars and, bingo, you just put eight hundred dollars in your wallet. But this is only the beginning. My company is manufacturing these sets for every university in the state. For every student you are able to recruit to join your business team we will give you five percent of their total sales."

"Do you have a calculator? Suppose you get ten other students to join, and they each sell only the eighty original sets they order. Of course, we are being very conservative. Once your sales team gets a taste of how easy it is to sell this product and the enormous profits they receive, they'll continue to sell far more than the original eighty. But suppose they only sell the first allotment. On the sales of only ten students you make a clear profit of two thousand dollars."

"Chet, this thing could become a gold mine. An organization with forty students selling for you all over the state could make you thousands. Why not get in on the ground floor? Take advantage of this, and in a year you'll be making so much you might debate whether you actually need that college degree to make it big in the business world. Wilson, here, turned down an executive position when he graduated from Princeton. He was making a lot more from the sales organization he built up in college than they offered him in salary."

"We just signed up your friend Fred in the next room. I can see why he's a business major. He seizes windows of opportunity when they come."

Harry pulled Fred's check for eight hundred dollars out of his wallet. "Chet, tonight you could plant a small seed that would have the potential of growing big bucks for you! Even if you don't have the money saved why not charge it on your Visa or Mastercard! It's a sure thing. We'll be glad to take either a check or credit card. Which would be better for you?"

Chet looked at the checkbook on his desk, then at the open grammar book. "Thanks, Harry, but not tonight! Your five minutes was more like twenty and I've got to study!"

The drug-pushing criminal we met in the last chapter is not the only enemy who seeks to seduce our kids into the danger zone of instant wealth. Proverbs also exposes the congenial, smooth-talking "Harry Hustler." A member of the Demolition Crew (Chapter 3), Harry is one manifestation of the moral dullard. He comes with a briefcase full of get-rich-quick stings and bad debts.

The Exposure of the Sting

A good-for-nothing, a trouble-maker—
    this is the individual who goes about with a crooked
        mouth,
    who winks his eyes,
    shuffles his feet,
    and signals with his fingers.
    His heart twists morality.
    Constantly he devises malicious schemes, and sows
        strife.

Therefore disaster will overtake him unexpectedly.
In a moment he will be broken, and there will be no
   healing.

                              (6:12–15)

His Characteristics (6:12–14)

The identifying distinctives of con men remain remarkably the same across time. We need to alert our kids to his perverted mouth, his deceptive body language, and his malicious schemes so that they will be protected from financial and personal ruin.

Whenever an individual's talk contradicts the financial principles of Proverbs, the red lights will blink on in the mind of the committed, wise individual. He will not succumb to the smooth tongue of the super-salesperson who suggests devious, effortless routes to wealth and fortune (cf. 4:24–27). The Harry Hustlers in life always speak with a "forked tongue." They lie, and our children should not be "babes in toyland" regarding them. We need to teach them about the false advertising, the sting operations, and high-sounding promises they will encounter in the marketplace. Hustlers twist the truth, and we must train our kids to be on guard against their schemes. They must be wary when promises are too good to be true.

Our children must also be trained to penetrate the hustler's disguise by being alert to his deceptive body language. They must beware of individuals who will not look at you right in the eye. In young teens this body language often reveals only a lack of confidence; however, the shifty eyes of the con man indicate not low self-esteem but the treachery of a rotten heart (6:13, 10:10). The eyes are the windows of the soul. Therefore we must teach our children to look people in the eye. When someone cannot meet their gaze with calmness and ease, they should be wary; possibly there are ulterior motives at work.

Harry Hustler's deceptive body language does not end with his eyes; his feet and hands also get into his act. When someone is trying to sell you something and he constantly shifts his feet and seems to be signaling with his hands, proceed with caution. Remember the kids' game, "I had my fingers crossed behind my back!" which supposedly invalidated what he promised with his mouth? The con artist never grows out of this lying trick. He winks mischievously at his partner as they seek to bait their pigeon. If we train our kids concerning the subtleties of deceptive body language, they will have the skills to avoid being someone's dupe.

Worldly-wise kids are taught that there is an enemy in the marketplace who lies with his mouth, who deceives with his body, and who uses his mind to constantly carve out malicious scams that harm the unsuspecting (6:14). Parents may inoculate their kids against the masters of intrigue by specifically interacting with their children. They must tell them about the illegality of "chain letters," which promise thousands to the recipient who passes the letter on and sends a few dollars to the addresses in the back. They must warn them of the frauds that plague any business community. These frauds coldly and mercilessly calculate ways to destroy their neighbors (24:8, cf. 11:9, 12:5, 20; 16:27, 30; 21:10). Kids can learn how to counteract this scheming with careful plans of their own, which will foster not deception, but peace and prosperity (12:20).

His Product (6:15)

The hustler promises a quick, effortless profit, but the bottom line is always the same—*strife*. The con feigns friendship and then abuses the relationship for his own selfish profit. This trickery generates in its victim an intense desire for revenge that will not easily be quenched (18:19). The resulting quarrels and lawsuits have the explosive power of pulverized charcoal being thrown on glow-ing embers (26:21). The hustler's end will always be the same. The fox may have pockets lined with money, but the baying hounds will eventually have him up a tree (6:15).

The individual who lives to make a profit by deceiving others deceives himself in the end. Sudden destruction is Harry Hustler's final bottom line. Often his tricks break the law of the land, and he ends up facing the sword of government (24:21–22). The hus-tler who refuses to listen to God's warnings will always be cut off by divine retribution, and there will be no one left to restore and heal. In the end no one hustles God.

A few of our kids will face economic ruin because we did not warn them about the hustler's tricks. But far more of them will be seduced by the bondage of easy credit.

The Slavery of Debt

The rich rule over the poor,
and the borrower is the lender's slave. (22:7)

When I first moved to Dallas in the early seventies, it was the invincible city with oil resources piping gallons of dollars into the economy. In the eighties the plummeting price of oil turned off the flow. The entire nation knows of the savings and loan failures, the real estate crashes, and the personal bankruptcies. We have been forced to face the fragility of providing for our daily needs. Jesus did not teach idle words when he taught us to pray, "Give us this day our daily bread."

Our heavenly Father is a gracious provider, but He is also a practical, effective economics professor. We can pray about natur-al crises that rob our table of food. The graciousness of others in such times of need can get us back to our feet. Bad speculative debts also steal our necessities, but people are not nearly as willing to rescue us out of holes we dig for ourselves.

To a generation that only asks, "Can I make the monthly payments?" Proverbs has some hard-nosed advice about debt. Wise parents take the time to share this wisdom with their kids. The mathematics of debt is not advanced calculus, yet few parents give their kids the simple facts about compound interest and the Architect's warning against foolish cosigning and borrowing.

Beware! Foolish Cosigning Can Cost You the Shirt off Your Back

> The individual who guarantees to cover the indebtedness of someone he does not know well will suffer for it, but whoever hates to enter into this type of agreement will be secure. (11:15)

> A person lacks common sense who co-signs for another, who assumes legal responsibility for someone else's debts. (17:18)

Proverbs repeatedly warns against pledging to cover another's debt. This is especially foolish when you have not had the time to discern whether the individual you are certifying is reliable. We need to warn our children about "friends" who beg them to cosign on the dotted line so they can procure a loan. Our kids need to remember who will be left with the monthly payments when their friend defaults.

Even worse is the man who gets involved with an immoral woman and then assumes responsibility for her indebtedness. He deserves to lose his shirt (20:16, 27:13). We must talk with our sons about the destructive financial entanglements that result from a romantic involvement with loose women. She'll purr like a kitten in his lap, but her claws will tear a hole in his bank account. In chapter 10 we'll discover that she robs him of far more than money.

Usually the wise person is cool, calm, and collected. But when he or she makes a mistake and rashly shakes hands on a foolish deal, he must go and frantically pester the individuals involved until he is released from the potentially disastrous obligation (6:1–5).

We must remember—proverbs are not commands but principles that depend upon the circumstances for their application. At times, cosigning a note is a wise and kind course of action. I'm thankful for established business people who gave me the opportunity to begin establishing a good credit rating as a young man. They did not, however, put their basic assets at risk, and they spent the personal time with me necessary to make a judgment about my dependability.

The wise parents of Proverbs had witnessed enough disasters to warn their kids about the hazards of foolish cosigning. On the other hand, they encouraged them to lend freely to legitimate companions and to be generous givers. Though God's children need to be reluctant about assuming responsibility for the debts of others, they need to be quick to lend or give to those in need (14:21, 19:17, 27:10). In the Old Testament God does not allow His children to exact interest from one another when money was needed to relieve serious financial difficulty (Exodus 22:25, Leviticus 25:35–37). In the New Testament Jesus instructs us to be willing to lend even to our enemies without expecting repayment. He promised to greatly reward this expression of His Father's merciful generosity (Luke 6:34–35).

Instead of going to the bank and cosigning a note when a fellow believer has a need, why not freely decide how much we can give and expect no repayment? How many brothers and sisters in church families are enemies today because they did not heed this common sense approach from Proverbs?

Assuming responsibility for someone else's debts is stupid. Losing your freedom because of your own debts is tragic.

Beware! Debt Enslaves

The rich rule over the poor,
and the borrower is the lender's slave. (22:7)

Few eighteen-year-olds going out into the world genuinely believe in the power of compound interest. When looking at the sleek lines of a new sports car, few young people consider its actual total cost. Their calculations analyze only whether they can scrape together the $364 necessary to make the monthly payments. Somehow they never look at the objective numbers. A five-year loan to pay for a $16,000 sports car at a periodic interest rate of 1.08 percent will cost $5,843 in interest. The total bill is not $16,000 but $21,843. If he earns $500 a week, he will work 11 1/2 weeks just to pay his lending institution for the privilege of borrowing.

When our kids charge $1,578.01 on a credit card in one year, at a periodic interest rate of 1.67 percent, and make monthly payments totaling $410 for the year, they will still owe $1,255.96, and pay $87.95 in interest. When you consider that the average American family has not one credit card but three or four, you can easily discern how a young couple falls into the credit-card trap. We need to help our kids to objectively face the burden of compound interest working against them.

My dad never sat down and showed me on paper how interest payments escalated. Before the days of computers it was far more difficult to print out this kind of data. Today I would encourage every parent to sit down with their children and show them exactly how much interest they will pay before they decide whether or not to buy something on credit. This is the negative side of compound interest.

Our children must also be exposed to the power of interest when, instead of borrowing, they are saving. At an annual interest rate of 8 percent, an initial investment of $10,000 will increase to $14,898 in five years, $22,196 in ten years, $33,069 in fifteen years, and $49,268 in twenty years. Every financial adviser can show us figures like this.

Few are wise enough to discipline themselves to save regularly. This explains why most families work a good proportion of every year simply to pay interest to credit institutions. The math is simple and objective, but the discipline to defer purchases until we can afford them and to save consistently is an inestimably valuable skill. Our kids will never learn it unless we parents take a hard look at the figures and at our priorities. Credit is easy but it ends in chains. Saving is difficult but it leads to power and freedom. Many of today's young adults never had parents who cared enough to teach these practical insights into personal finance. This can become a powerful doorway of ministry.

Mary and I have friends in Indiana who since their retirement after a successful career in business spend time counseling couples about the dangers of debt, the power of a budget, and the blessings that can come when biblical principles of finance are followed. Remember, we learned in Proverbs chapter one that the mature, wise person never retires from the responsibility of passing on life skills to the next generation. Why don't some of you who have learned some tough lessons about money pass along these survival techniques to others?

Five weeks after Chet's confrontation with Harry and Wilson, he was again studying at his desk. A "B" on the midterm test was acceptable, but he was beginning to learn the system, and an "A" was not out of reach by the time finals rolled round. He answered a knock at his door.

"Chet, can I come in for a minute?"

"Sure Fred. How are things going?"

"Not too well! Remember those executive types who came through the dorm about a month ago?"

"Yeah, they told me you got in on the ground floor of a great profit-making bonanza. Let me see one of the pen and pencil sets they sent you!"

Fred grimaced, "That's what I came to ask you about. They cashed my check, but I never received a thing. I called the number on their business card, and they never heard of any Harry with a pen-and-pencil business. Do you have any ideas about how I can get back my $800? I need it to stay in school next semester."

Think About It

A business professor shared how a sharp enterpriser earned a bundle when everyone was thinking about solar energy. He took out an ad in the major papers—"Solar Dryer—Just $48.98! Everything you need!"

He included a post office box, and the checks and orders poured in. The people received their orders, much to their chagrin—a clothesline and pins worth about $3. Nothing illegal was done and the entrepreneur made a killing.

With your family, use the principles learned in this chapter to discuss why it would be wrong to use this type of business idea even though it made you a great deal of money?

7

The Sluggard

Saturday morning our garage was in chaos, an eloquent testimony to the Second Law of Thermodynamics. The time had come to inject some energy into the system and move it back from the brink of total disorder. So I began sweeping and shoveling the dirt. In their room my two teenage sons slept till late in the morning, then sat around reading.

Sneezing and coughing in the mushroom cloud of dust, I thought about my two strong young men cooling it inside. *Jonathan and Joel, you should know I need your help*, I murmured to myself. *Kids! Mention a good time—they're pulsating with energy. Face them with a dirty garage—and they need their sleep.*

My anger began to boil as I cleaned alone. *If they can't see what needs to be done, it's not worth asking them!*

At the critical point I slammed the broom to the floor and rushed inside. "Did you guys ever think I might need some help?" I grabbed another Kleenex® and sneezed. "All you do is think about yourselves." This onslaught of verbal gunfire strafed them in total surprise.

Later that day when I had cooled down, I went to them and apologized. When you are growing six or eight inches every few months and your week includes a complex juggling act of balancing athletics, piano practice, homework assignments, and church youth group activities, you do need extra sleep. Jonathan and Joel were not maliciously taking advantage of me. I needed to remind myself that the person who internally seethes but refuses to directly ask others for help will always end up doing things alone.

It is a medical fact that young people need more sleep than adults. Parents must put this given into the equation for raising them wisely. On the other hand, we must also recognize that the individual who sleeps daily until 10:00, becomes an expert on game shows and soap operas, spends the afternoon in a cafe drinking coffee and spinning yarns with his buddies, and boasts about all he is going to accomplish is becoming enslaved to the addictive tranquilizer called "Laziness." Proverbs exposes the disposition and destiny of Sam Sluggard. We can laugh at his humorous antics, but our kids must be alerted to the paralyzing consequences of becoming a "couch potato."

Two Cartoons

The lazy man does not roast his game,
but diligence is a man's precious wealth. (12:27)

The lazy man buries his hand in the dish.
He is too tired to return it to his mouth. (26:15, cf. 19:24)

With satire the writer of Proverbs first pictures the sluggard as a lethargic hunter. Even if he does muster the energy to bag his game, he runs out of gas before a proper fire is kindled, and his game is not roasted. In contrast to the diligent individual, he never tastes the succulent rewards of his success. He's too lazy to cook his own meat.

The second verbal cartoon takes us to an oriental meal. Instead of sitting on chairs at a table, the custom in ancient Israel was to recline on the floor and dip into a common dish. Visualize a group of teens eating chips and dip on your living room floor while watching videos, and you've got a good approximation to the scene of Proverbs 19:24. Sam Sluggard is so lazy he falls asleep with his hand in the dish. Everyone snickers as French onion dip oozes between his listless fingers. In the midst of the laughter, Proverbs provokes us to take a serious look at ourselves and evaluate how many of the termites of laziness are already eating away at our life structures.

The Lazy Disposition

The couch potato detests work, but he loves to sleep, to talk, to dream, and to excuse.

Dangerous Slumber

If you expect to harvest, you must plant. If you expect to reap success, you must plant the seeds. The wise son plants his seeds. The lazy son disappoints his father by sleeping through the planting season and missing the moment of opportunity (10:5). At harvest time, filled with optimism, he expects to share the rewards with the sowers. But crops will not grow from his unsown ground (20:4). Intelligence, talent, and opportunity do not yield success while he pulls the covers up, and rolls over in bed like a door on a hinge (26:14). The father's admonition is simple, but strong. "Do not love sleep, lest you be reduced to poverty; open your eyes, and you will eat well" (20:13).

These words convict me at 5:45 a.m. when I am tempted to hit the snooze button on the clock radio, *Fifteen more minutes of precious relaxation, the most cherished sleep of the night,* I say to myself. A swift kick from Mary jars me to reality. "It's time to get up and get planting."

Our children must be trained to respond to alarm clocks. If they do not, it could someday cost them their jobs. Companies tolerate only so many tardy slips. How many college degrees have been forfeited simply because a student consistently did not get up to the alarm so he or she could be on time for class? "The door turns on its hinges, the sluggard turns over in his bed" (26:14).

Empty Talk

When the sluggard is awake, instead of working, he is gabbing. His mouth is filled with exciting stories about what he is going to do. Nothing is wrong with Sam's appetite for prosperity. He covets the rewards hard work can bring. What he lacks is the will to work hard (13:3–4). Consequently, the frustration of unfulfilled longings will be the death of him (21:25–26). In Chapter 15 we will face the awesome power of words, but words are impotent when they are not connected to a person's feet. "In all hard work there will be abundant profit, but mere talk brings nothing but need" (14:23).

Impossible Dreams

When you first meet Sam Sluggard, he impresses you with a dazzling array of opportunities that await him. If athletics captures his interest at the moment, you will hear of his past exploits and the million-dollar professional contracts he could sign. If the conversation turns to business, he becomes the erudite stock broker with inside tips for investing and cunning strategies for marketing a new product. He is an expert on everything. If you don't believe it, ask him (26:16).

This explains why Sam cannot keep a job. His employers never appreciate his worth to the company, he claims. Often he must quit because another dream has beckoned. This is the "big one" he's been waiting for all his life. In desperation, his family follows him from one place to another as he pursues his impossible dream. In reality, the dream is a nightmare as he flees from his creditors.

Proverbs is not demeaning the importance of dreams, especially for the young. A friend of mine, Tonya Crevier, is barely five feet tall. As a teenager she dreamed of becoming a basketball player. Everyone mocked this short girl's goal, but, unlike the sluggard, her talk was not mere fantasy. She practiced for hours on her ball-handling and shooting. She developed an incredible ability to spin a basketball on her fingertips. Her skills at ball-handling and passing enabled her to star in high-school and college ball. Today she earns her living spinning basketballs for thousands during NBA half times as one of the world's preeminent ball-handlers. Proverbs speaks not against dreams, but against a failure to develop one's available resources.

> The one who works their ground will be satisfied with bread,
>   but the person who chases fantasies lacks any sense.
>
>   (12:11)

> They will be filled with poverty. (28:19)

These Proverbs present more than common sense for farmers. God gives all of us a plot of ground—our talents. We must cultivate our potentials by discipline and practice. Laziness is not a joke. It is the sinful failure to invest our God-given abilities and use them to be productive for Him. Laziness buries this precious bag of gold in a hole of wild excuses. The Creator's anger burns against this waste (Matthew 25:14–30).

Paralyzing Fears

When you ask the couch potato why he did not go out and check all the "help wanted" classified leads you cut out of the Sunday paper for him, he replies, "There is a lion outside, I could be murdered in the middle of the marketplace" (22:13, cf. 26:13).

Wild excuses and irrational fears throw a pretense of legitimacy over the sluggard's failure to get going and find a job. His excuse was not as far-fetched in ancient Israel as it would be in our society. Lions did prowl the land, but hardly on crowded streets.

However, drugs, muggings, the hazards of driving on the freeway, and a bad economy represent the "lions" of the modern world your lazy offspring, relative, or friend might use to explain why he cannot go out and hunt for work. He will, however, allow you to go out in the danger zone to put bread on the table and a roof over his head. Wild excuses are the trademark of laziness.

The Products of Laziness

Laziness produces undependability, restricted options, and finally enslaving poverty. "Like vinegar setting the teeth on edge, or smoke stinging the eyes, so is the sluggard to those who send him to fulfill a responsibility" (10:26).

In contrast to the reliable individual who brings refreshment to those who trust him because of his skill in carrying out the responsibility, the sluggard produces agony for those who depend upon him. His job never gets completed. He procrastinates, makes wild excuses, and gets distracted. Like the hare in the fable, he falls asleep in the clover patch while the dependable tortoise faithfully wins the race. "The way of the sluggard is like a hedge of thorns, but the path of the upright is an unimpeded highway" (15:19).

Laziness causes one to throw away the opportunities of youth, thus leading to restricted options in adulthood. Bad grades in high school limit the couch potato's options for college. Partying and oversleeping in the first semester of community college yield probation slips and expulsion after finals. Powerful friends provide a good-paying labor job for their lazy young friend. They feel sorry for him and give him another opportunity. He needs time to mature and get his feet on the ground, they say. But after showing up late for his shift three times and then asking the boss for vacation time, he lands jobless back in his room at Dad and Mom's. Sponging off his parents protects him for a time from being beaten up by the villain of poverty (6:10–11).

God graciously cares for those trapped in poverty by ill health, natural disaster, or other tragic circumstances. He commands His children to be generous to the needy (14:21, 31). On the other hand, God does say those who refuse to follow the example of the ant and work hard to provide for themselves (6:6–8) or those who neglect to cultivate their abilities and sow their opportunities (20:5, 24:32–34) do not deserve to be fed. Paul remembered this practical advice when he counseled the Thessalonians about idlers, busybodies, and moochers: "If anyone will not work, neither will they eat" (2 Thessalonians 3:10). Hunger is one teacher who might be able to get through to Sam Sluggard and arouse him from his deadly slumber.

If lazy tendencies continue, the sluggard will lose his freedom to enslaving poverty (10:4, 12:24). Before our kids submit to such bondage, we must give them the cure for lethargy.

The Cure for Sluggard's Disease

The parent following the Learn-and-Live model of parenting knows that an intense exposure to reality is a major factor in communicating values. If children are lazy, they need to see the effects of laziness fleshed out in life. The previous section contains common sense ideas. The problem with common sense, however, is that we assume everyone has it, so we don't bother to spell things out clearly for the younger generation. We must raise our children in a home where Sam Sluggard is viewed as a violent thief who desires to rob them of their talents and opportunities (6:10–11).

They do not have to be enslaved by irrational fears. They can commit their efforts to the Architect and know that He will bring everything to a successful conclusion (16:3, 9). This confidence provides the motivation to diligently plan and pursue goals (10:4, 14:23, 21:5). With trust in the Lord we can develop our available resources. He can teach us priorities—to be willing to put off the consumption of wealth until the means for generating wealth have been put into place. You do not go out and buy a house on mortgage and then go looking for a job (24:27). God can teach His child diligence as he learns to observe the bustling activities of His tiny creatures, such as ants and bees (6:6–8).

A mother screams at her kids about their clothes thrown all over the room, but continues to pick up after them. A dad angrily demands that his twenty-four-year-old son move out of the house and find a job but continues to make payments on his son's sports car and gas credit card. The couch potato needs to be fried—he must experience the painful effects of his laziness. Only then will he be willing to enter the school of diligence and industry.

My garage is filthy again. It's time to wake up Jonathan, Joel, Joshua, and Jenae. We can make a family project of overcoming the chaos by some diligent sweeping.

Think About It

1. Study, work, and play—many feel that you are to play when you are a small child, study during your school years, work during the young and middle adult years, and then return to play in retirement. The wise individual recognizes that these three need to be part of life at every stage. Think through your family's weekly schedule. Is there a balance between study, work, and play? What are some changes that need to be made to achieve the balance?

2. Children need to learn the connection between diligence and success, between laziness and failure. After going over the principles in this chapter, see if you and your children can come up with real-life illustrations from the news or from your own experiences that illustrate these principles.

8

Skillful Money Management

If you have not been trustworthy in handling worldly
wealth, who will trust you with true riches?

(Luke 16:11 NIV)

We can warn our kids against the seduction of the criminal
gang, the tricks of the sting, and the sluggard's deadly slumber, but they cannot graduate from the Wisdom School of Finance
until they know the value of the dollar, the threats it can bring,
and how to shrewdly spend their heavenly Father's dollars.

The Value of Money

With hard-headed realism, Proverbs answers the question,
"How much is our money worth?" Some security, some friends,
and some power.

Security

> The wealth of the rich is their fortified city,
>> but the terrifying ruin of the poor is their poverty.
>> (10:15)

Who has more serenity when another bill arrives in the mailbox—the individual with thirty thousand dollars in CDs tucked
away in the bank, or someone who has already used all of next
week's paycheck to make minimum payments on his credit cards?
Landing in a hospital bed causes trauma for everyone. But fears
greatly increase when you cannot afford health insurance. To live

111

from one week to the next worrying how to feed your family is frightening. The next meal is hardly a concern for the wealthy. Proverb's point is obvious: poverty brings terror, and a savings account provides some sense of security. Proverbs goes on to tell our kids the whole truth—wealth does bring a measure of security, but it is never secure. It can be attacked by circumstances beyond one's control, sprout wings, and fly away (18:11, 23:5).

When the oil crisis struck Houston, high-rolling yuppies, living in posh, upper-class neighborhoods, went into their bankers' offices to surrender the keys to their homes and their expensive cars. With no jobs, how could they continue to make their payments? Money can never give us a piece of the Rock. God alone is a strong Gibraltar. The wise individual trusts in Him and finds a durable security.

Friends

The poor man is hated even by his companions,
but those who love the rich are many. (14:20)

The friend who never has enough money to pick up his tab at a restaurant but expects you to cover for him will not be your friend for long. The tendency to mooch off the generosity of others destroys one's opportunity to develop healthy, mature relationships. Even members of your family begin to dread your appearance when you always come with your palm up (19:7). Our children need to be taught to pay their own way.

At times friends will graciously pay the bill, and we need to receive this with thankfulness. We must, however, warn our children against beginning to expect this. As a pastor this was an important lesson for me to learn. Closeness with others cannot be built if you constantly expect them to give you special treatment because you are a minister. Pastors who ask for their clergy discount, discount their reputation in a community. We must all learn the art of knowing when to carry someone else's burden, when to allow someone to carry ours, and when to carry our own (Galatians 6:2–5).

Though chronic need is a friendship repellent, money in the wallet attracts a crowd. If you have a box at the stadium and can invite others to the games, if you can afford to pick up the tab at fancy restaurants, and if you can pay for others to accompany you on exotic vacations, you will not lack for company. Jesus Himself taught us to win friends with generosity, graciously forgiving debts and using money to meet the needs of others (Luke 16:9–10). Because the Master loves to cancel debts, the individual who reflects this divine characteristic will be welcomed into his eternal home (Luke 16:9). The individual who manipulates people will face the opposite destiny.

Money does win friends and influence people. But what kind of friends does it win? If you're wealthy, the threat is that using your money, rather than true desire for participation in your life, can become the basis of relationships. The prodigal son learned in the school of hard knocks that when the cash is gone, so are the companions. Alone, we discover we were being used, not loved.

Power

> The rich rule over the poor. (22:7a)

Money is power. Proverbs tells it like it is. The wealthy make the investments, set the interest rates, and lobby the government. Poor people must become experts in using words to win the favor of their benefactors. The powerful rich brusquely say whatever they please without worrying about how it will be taken (18:23). On the other hand, the affluent often forget there is an ultimate Judge who is not impressed with their money (11:4, cf. James 1:10–11).

Money has value, but not in the end. Wisdom is practical: wealth has some worth, but there are nine possessions money cannot buy.

Values More Valuable Than Money

My brother Ron is three years younger than I. I remember, as kids, carrying on intense negotiations with him over money. On his birthday one year, he opened a card from one of our relatives, and a dollar bill was tucked inside. Opportunity knocked for his "worldly-wise" eight-year-old brother. Holding a shiny dime in his face, my line would begin, "Ron, it's too bad they just gave you a piece of paper. Wouldn't you rather have this nice, shiny money? It will last much longer. Look! You can't tear it. Since it's your birthday, I'll trade you even."

My five-year-old brother would take the dime every time. His naiveté about the value of money enabled me to cheat him until Dad and Mom discovered my duplicity and put an end to my hustling career. Our children will lose far more than a dollar bill if we fail to teach them nine values in life always worth more than money:

1. Wisdom

Always choose wisdom over money because it can give you a long, pleasant life and the ability to generate prosperity (3:13–18). When our teenagers ask us if they can work long hours at a fast-food restaurant to pay for a new pickup and their grades drop below passing, we need to talk with them about whether we are trading dollars for dimes. Their options in the sophisticated modern marketplace will be limited if they waste their opportunity to get an education (8:10–11, 16:16).

2. Righteousness

Always choose obedience to God's standards revealed in His Word over money. When He evaluates our lives, moral character, not money, will be vital (11:4). Materialism offers no reliable bank and trust. God alone is worth our trust (11:28). The person who pursues wealth bankrupts his soul eternally (Luke 12:13–21). The person who hungers and thirsts for conformity to God's standards ends up walking on what the wealthy lived their lives for, for gold is the gravel of heaven. "Blessed are those who hunger and thirst for righteousness, for they will be filled" (Matthew 5:6 NIV).

3. Reverence

Always choose to revere the Lord rather than to make a profit. When money becomes a god, trouble becomes a way of life (15:16). If we adore God, we end up gaining wealth, honor, and life (22:4).

4. Love

Always choose genuine closeness with others over lavishly gratifying your physical desires. Eating Cherrios® with loved ones who care is better than eating prime rib with those who hate you (15:17). In my third year of college I was a newlywed, and I remember eating crackers and peanut butter because our money for the month was gone. But Mary's love turned crackers into steak. We all know money cannot purchase love. If we have love, we are far richer than the one who has only money. Ultimately, the person who receives God's love has both love and prosperity (21:21).

5. Humility

Always choose to build your sense of value on the fact that you are made in God's image, rather than pretend that the possession of money makes you worth something. When faced with the choice to high-roll it with the proud, "self-made" materialists, or make do with those who possess nothing but moral and spiritual values, choose the humble team. This is God's team and His team always wins (16:18–19). Moses, the founder of the Israelite nation, knew this and became immortal (Hebrews 11:26–27). Like the righteous lovers, the humble receive even wealth in the end (22:4). "Blessed are the meek, for they will inherit the earth" (Matthew 5:5 NIV).

6. Peace

Always choose peace over prosperity. Eating crusty old bread in peace and quiet is better than banqueting in splendor with hostility and strife. The gleam in the glamorous festivities of the rich is often the glint of steel off a hidden dagger that will cut your throat (17:1). Those who live for power and prestige produce discord, not harmony. "Blessed are the peacemakers, for they will be called the sons of God" (Matthew 5:9 NIV).

7. Integrity

Always choose to remain ethically blameless over becoming rich through illicit means (19:1, 28:6). To remain spiritually sound is more valuable than causing your entire personality to become diseased because you cheated to get rich. "Blessed are the pure in heart, for they will see God" (Matthew 5:8 NIV).

8. Truthfulness

Always choose to be an honest poor man rather than a rich liar (19:22). Our lives need to model dependability. Many say, "You can count on me!" Few mean it (20:6). When things get tough the unfaithfulness of the liar hurts more than an abscessed tooth (25:19). Our children need to be taught to place a high price tag on the truth.

9. Reputation

Always choose to maintain a good name over maintaining a large bank account (22:1). Our character gives us far more weight in a community than our money. The chieftains of the Colombian drug cartel can use their money to build massive mansions in Medellin, with manicured lawns, six-stall garages, and helipads, but their dirty money cannot purchase a good name.

Esteem is priceless and delicate. Our kids need to face reality— a reputation built over a lifetime can collapse in a moment. President Nixon's name is synonymous with Watergate, not with the opening of relations with China. Already a child is building a name for himself, either good or bad (20:11). Jesus' actions as a boy won him favor with God and man (Luke 2:52). In collecting funds the apostle Paul maintained proper accounting procedures to guard against any criticism (2 Corinthians 8:20–21). A good reputation with outsiders, not the giving power of the donor, was the first qualification of leadership in the first-century church (1 Timothy 3:2, 7).

Choices are not complicated in Proverbs, but they are critical. Whenever our kids face the decision—wisdom, righteousness, reverence, love, humility, peace, integrity, truthfulness, and reputation, versus money—they need to place the higher price tag on the former values. Not to do so is greed—the idolatrous worship of things over the humble adoration of our Creator (Ephesians 5:5). Greed brings nothing but trouble (15:27). By displaying these proper values in our own lives we can train our children not to trade dollars for dimes.

The Hazards of Money

Advertisers trigger our children's dreams about all the fun their products can bring. Who challenges them to stop and think about some of the safety hazards that accompany all the stuff money can buy?

Have they considered that with affluence come threats from thieves, kidnappers, and blackmailers? Of course the rich can afford Doberman guard dogs, alarm systems, impenetrable walls, and locked iron gates to protect their estate from enemies. Should they be kidnapped, they can pay the ransom. On the other hand a poor man doesn't need an alarm system. Who wants to bother with extorting money from one who has none (13:8)? When there's nothing to lose, who cares if you lose it? Few stop and consider that being poor has some advantages.

Making money is a life-threatening addiction. The love of money places an individual on the "just one more dollar" treadmill, a stress test that will not turn off until your heart breaks. We need to warn our kids against destroying their health trying to make it big (23:4). Just when you think you have it made the stock market crashes and you must return to "Go" to begin the climb all over again.

We need to pray with our children for the golden mean, "Give us today our daily bread." Too little bread and we can be driven to steal, thus shaming our God. Too much bread and pride can cause us to say, Who needs God? (30:7–9; cf. Job 21:13–16). There are no self-made men or women. Worldly-wise kids understand the three hazards of money worship—the threat of kidnap, the threat of physical collapse, and the threat of spiritual collapse. On the positive side they need to learn how to spend their Heavenly Daddy's money wisely.

Priorities in Using Our Heavenly Dad's Money

"David, here's my wallet," my dad would say. "Ride your bike downtown and pick up a loaf of bread and milk for Mom."

I still remember the pride I felt when Dad handed me his thick leather wallet stuffed with bills—to a ten-year-old, fifteen ones seemed like a fortune. The fact that Dad trusted me with his wallet on a trip to the store meant a great deal to me. This trust helped me resist the temptation to buy a that big Baby Ruth at the pharmacy or one of those model airplanes that beckoned from the craft store. When we grow up we must realize that a greater Father entrusts us with His resources. We will get our priorities right in purchasing when we realize our heavenly Daddy has entrusted us with His wallet. In order of importance, here are four guidelines that have helped me to spend God's way.

1. Honor Him with your money. (3:9–10)

Once a year at income tax time we have to prepare a thorough accounting of our money for the government. Go into your files and retrieve last year's readout of expenditures. Carefully observe where your money was spent. This gives an objective indication of the things that are important in your life. More important than percentages, Proverbs teaches us to esteem God with each of our dollars. We must not give him ten percent and then feel free to do with the rest whatever we please since we have paid our dues. An accountant should be able to look at our entire budget and conclude that God is given weighty consideration in our lives (3:9–10). Where we invest our treasure is the true location of our heart (Luke 12:34).

From the toddler stage our children should be trained to give to help relieve the hard times of fellow Christians as an expression of their love for God (1 John 3:16–18; 2 Corinthians 8:9, 13), and to tangibly honor the importance of the gospel and the teaching of God's Word by their support of those engaged in this ministry (Galatians 6:6). Their giving should be consistent and in proportion to God's provision for them (1 Corinthians 16:2; 2 Corinthians 9:6). We need to challenge them to think, *How can I honor God with my allowance?* When they begin to work they can continue to value the Lord in their giving.

2. Meet the material needs of your family.

Credit cards should not be used to fake a higher lifestyle than you can afford when there is not enough money to pay for necessities (12:9, 13:7). Wise people settle down, earn the bread they eat, and live within their means (2 Thessalonians 3:12). God places a high value on meeting the needs of one's family (1 Timothy 5:8). The good man values these money management principles; therefore, he is usually blessed with far more than his necessities. His savings bring benefit even to his grandchildren (13:22).

3. Graciously give to those in need.

Wise people do not feed couch potatoes, but they do feed those who are suffering in poverty (14:21). Generosity to the needy honors the Lord. The individual who pridefully insults the poor and increases their oppression will face the anger of their Defender (14:31).

When Joshua was in second grade he revealed some of the values coming through to him in this spelling piece he did for school:

"If I were a farmer, I would plant wheat for my crop. I would use it to make bread to feed the birds and me. I would sale [sic] it to raise money for my stuff. I would give some of my money and food that I raise to the poor people. And to rusia [sic]."

We worked with Josh on the peculiarities of English spelling. But, unlike the rich farmer in Jesus' story who only stored up "stuff" for himself (Luke 12), Joshua wants to give to meet the needs of others, including the Russians.

4. Enjoy with others the good things God gives you.

Because of God's kindness, those who follow the practical values of hard work and living within their means normally accumulate more than enough to provide their necessities. We honor God, not only by giving to the poor and to those who proclaim His Word, but also by using our abundance to bring joy to others. God alone can give satisfaction, the ability to enjoy the fruit of hard work (Ecclesiastes 2:24–25, 5:18–20; cf. 1 Timothy 6:17–19). Godly parents warn against both the pride of possessions and the pride of privation. Neither opulence or asceticism pleases our heavenly Daddy. He wants us to use the money in His wallet to honor and enjoy Him and to meet the needs of ourselves and others.

Think About It

1. Family discussion: Have you ever heard the Bible quoted like this: "Money is the root of all evil"? Look up 1 Timothy 6:10 and read exactly what the apostle Paul actually said. What is the difference between saying money is the root of evil and saying that the love of money is a root of evil? What are some of the good things according to Proverbs that money can do for us?

2. Study the list of nine values that are more valuable than money. Think of some concrete examples in life where the choice could be money over one of these values. Explain why money would be the wrong choice.

3. Go ahead and dig out last year's income tax records. Look carefully at how your family used its money and then jot down your priorities. Are there some things that need to be changed in order to reflect the priorities stressed in Proverbs for the use of money? Our children's values about money will be more strongly influenced by our actions than by our words.

Sex Blueprints

Cherish the intoxication of marital love;
hate the deception of illicit sex.

9

The Sex Teacher

If you have a teenager, you're accustomed to the perpetual ring of a telephone. For years the calls in our house were for me or my wife, but as soon as our older boys became teenagers, this changed dramatically. The ring of the telephone now meant, "Hello, is Jonathan or Joel there?" The calls came from some beautiful high-school girls, and they sent shock waves through my system. *How could sixteen-year-old girls be interested in my "little boys"?* I thought. But a quick look at my sons—now five inches taller than their dad, reminded me that they were hardly "little boys." They definitely had all the equipment to attract the opposite sex, and again I thought about the desirability of locking them up in a monastery for the next six years. Consider the temptations kids face today.

Researchers report that nearly 50 percent of the nation's ten million young women between the ages of fifteen and nineteen have premarital sex. Teen pregnancy bankrupts the country's welfare system as Congress debates reform. In April of 1987 *People* magazine caught the tragedy of this promiscuity with their cover story, "What's Gone Wrong with Teen Sex?" "In America 3,000 adolescents become pregnant each day. A million a year. Four out of five are unmarried. More than half get abortions, 'Babies having babies.' Or killing them" (April 13, 1987).

Our teenagers face incredible social pressure. Virginity is a "dirty little secret," the "responsible" way to stop the AIDS crisis is to use condoms, and sex is OK if done with someone you care about deeply. This promiscuous atmosphere pressures us to react, and it is tempting to resort to the monastery approach. But again, as in dealing with the enticement to take drugs, no walls are massive enough to ensure against the penetration of immorality. *The rigid, threatened approach could also rob our children of the free expression of sexual passion God intends for them to enjoy in marriage.*

Some evangelical parents confidently say, "This adolescent promiscuity is a problem for the secular humanists. Our kids are safe within the walls of sound, Bible-believing churches and Christian schools. Let's keep quiet about sex, and maybe our teens will innocently escape the magnetism of lust."

Sadly, this is never the case. I went to a Christian high school buried in the depths of central Florida's orange groves. We saw the outside world for a couple of weeks at Christmas and then not again until the summer. This isolation did not prevent immorality from infecting some of my classmates.

Because I do about fifteen hours of pastoral counseling each week, I frequently come into contact with Christian girls who are illegitimately pregnant or "born again" guys who admit that they cannot control their sexual passion. The statistics concerning immorality in the church are not significantly different from those in the secular world. The fall of some of the most outspoken defenders of sexual purity should caution anyone against believing he or she can escape to a place of safety, free from the threat of lust.

There is evidence to suggest, however, that some adults are wising up about immorality. A desire for intimacy, the secure fulfillment of faithful family living, and the reality that AIDS is not an itch, but death have caused the rebels of the sixties to become the conservatives of today. In 1984 *Time* magazine declared "The Revolution Is Over" and made this conclusion: "Most Americans seem stubbornly committed to family, marriage, and the traditional idea that sex is tied to affection or justified by it. 'Cool sex,' cut off from the emotions and the rest of life, seems empty, unacceptable, or immoral."

The movie *Fatal Attraction* made big bucks from the collective guilt of an adult generation that is learning that a one-night stand could be murder. But are teenagers tuning in to this newfound wisdom? The sexual health of the next generation depends upon our teenagers hearing the right sex educator, a communicator with the courage to expose the tragedy of sexual immorality and the ecstasy of passionate sexual fulfillment in marriage.

The Preeminent Sex Educator

Parents blush, Dr. Ruth chatters on, and the guys and girls in the locker rooms continue to boast about their exploits. Listen to some of the advice offered to teenagers from today's sex experts. When asked about the AIDS crisis, eminent Johns Hopkins sexologist Dr. John Money gave this solution: "What we should be doing as a society is giving very explicit and strongly positive messages to young people getting ready for puberty on the positive joys of masturbation . . . not general instruction, but very explicit teaching" (*Psychology Today*, May, 1988, p. 48). He blames our sexual problems on archaic religious ideas. The old morality represses scientists like himself from teaching the truth about sexual freedom.

I agree that religious tradition has often repressed legitimate sexual desire, but treating human sex as primate mating behavior is not the answer either. In the midst of this cacophony of advice, the father and mother of Proverbs offer the truth about healthy sexual behavior. Their instructions go far beyond biology to the crucial issue of how to motivate children to live morally. Here we find parents who accept their sex education responsibility, who know the divine truth about sexual behavior, and who seek to entice budding adolescent sexual desires toward wisdom, not foolishness. Their three sex talks begin with confidence.

Son, pay attention to my wisdom,
Open your ears to my understanding,
That you may follow well-considered sex practices
And that your lips may guard knowledge.

(5:1–2)

My son, observe your father's commandment
  And do not abandon your mother's teaching!
Continually bind them upon your heart.
  Clasp them around your neck.
Wisdom will guide you when you walk.
  She will watch over you when you lie down.
  She will speak to you when you awake.
For this commandment is a lamp
  And this teaching is light.
The way of life is found by heeding corrective
discipline that will protect you from the evil woman,
  from the smooth tongue of the woman of mystery.

(6:20–24)

My son, obey my words!
Treasure my commandments within you!
If you obey my commandments you will live.
  Guard my instructions as the apple of your eye.
Bind them on your fingers.
  Write them upon the tablet of your heart.
Say to wisdom, 'You are my sister!'
  Call understanding your intimate friend.
They will protect you from the sensual woman
  From the mysterious woman with her seductive words
of flattery.

(7:1–5)

The Parental Responsibility

Who needs a recent poll from *Time* to know that parental apathy is a major factor in creating the present "values vacuum"? More than 90 percent of those who responded to a *Time* survey agreed that morals have fallen because parents fail to take responsibility for their children or to imbue them with decent moral standards (May 25, 1987). We parents know that a social worker, a guidance counselor, or a pastor cannot replace us as the initial teachers of sexual relationships. The difficulty is getting the right messages across to our kids.

When reminded of our responsibility to talk to our children about sex, we tend to overreact. Painfully aware that our passion to get ahead often robs us of involvement in our kids' personal lives, we try to make up for lost time by delivering stern lectures. Dads especially love to be preachers. But this "preachy" mode is a turnoff for our children.

The scene begins with Dad's getting out his podium, dusting off the family Bible, sitting his kids down in orderly rows, and then eloquently delivering sermon number 46, "Sexual Purity." He forgets that the kids were looking forward to going out for pizza with their friends. Noticing their bored restlessness, he concludes that the younger generation has no interest in spiritual values.

The wise parents in Proverbs take a different tack. They did not begin with a sermon but with a relationship. They took the time to be personally involved in their son's life. Years later when he committed their teaching to writing, he reminisced about his childhood and concluded, "I was a son to my father, tenderly loved and unique in the heart of my mother" (4:3).

Here was a dad who did more than create a child. He fathered a son. He gave himself to his child. He invested the personal time the father-son relationship demands.

Here was a mom who affectionately treated each of her children as an individual. She made each one feel unique by the tender way she loved him or her.

Nothing is more important than time in building a relationship. Time to listen on the way to a soccer game. Time for sharing a special family night at a restaurant, and time for family vacations. Skillful parents know they must share their lives in order to share their values. They know that it is while they are relaxing on the grass after fishing for a couple of hours that the special opportunity to communicate with an eleven-year-old might present itself. The effective dad does not miss the moment.

"Son, when I was about your age a struggle began in my life. It dawned on me there were other beings on the planet besides boys. I felt powerful urges inside and wondered if some of these beautiful creatures called girls would ever want me. Some of the guys at school stole peeks at *Playboy*. Others began to boast about their sexual prowess. I had to ask myself how I felt about sex and lust, and how to deal with these powerful forces inside me. God's Word gave me the right answers. It helped me to know that I would enjoy sex in His time, according to His design, and they protected me from some serious mistakes. I want to pass on the truth about sex to you."

Parents who invest the time necessary to develop intimacy with their children take the most powerful step toward inoculating them against immorality. Good sex education begins with parents who have time to genuinely know their kids.

Though my own dad was an itinerant evangelist and director of a large youth organization, I am thankful that he had time for me. I remember him cheering me on at midget league football games Saturday morning at 9:00 though he had a live, nationwide radio broadcast to pull off at 7:30 Saturday night. He was there in the spring of my eighth-grade year when the opposing shortstop snagged three of my line drives, and we lost the baseball championship.

Mom was always there when I arrived home from school. I remember running up the stairs and into her bedroom. In spite of chronic health problems, she had time to chat about my day. She assured her husky ten-year-old that he would grow taller and thinner. Girls would become interested in him someday. My parents gave me more than preaching. They gave me themselves. Therefore I listened when Dad and Mom talked to me about the facts of life.

Relationship is the first priority. However, it is not enough. Our kids need right answers.

The Divine Answers

The parents of Proverbs gave more than time to their children. They gave inspired guidance. Observe how they refer to their teaching as *wisdom*, *understanding*, and *knowledge*. They exhort their kids to memorize and internalize their instructions. They make the claim that if their children will listen, they will enjoy safe sex. How can these parents be so confident that they know the true moral standards? Is this not parental arrogance?

If I spoke that way about my own personal authority, it would be pretentious. But Proverbs does not present merely human values. God breathes through the proverbial wisdom. It is not ancient personal opinion but the design plan for skillful sexual living, and it comes straight from the divine Architect's drawing board.

These sexual standards have been inherent in the created order for thousands of years for all cultures. If obeyed, they produce enjoyment. If broken, sexual life fractures. Just like the tablets of Moses and the revelation of the prophets, the wise man's counsel has the authority of the supreme Ruler of the universe. Proverbs' counsel is God's burning lamp, illuminating the path to healthy, fulfilling sexual relationships (cf. Proverbs 6:23; Psalm 119:105). In a society where the only absolute states that there are no absolutes, Proverbs challenges parents to decide whether their authority will be Dr. Ruth, Dr. Money, the latest poll in *Cosmopolitan,* or the enduring divine revelation recorded in the Scriptures.

In *The Closing of the American Mind,* Dr. Allan Bloom argues against the modern dictum that "all things are relative" and challenges America to return to the "fundamental principles" and to "moral virtues."* I contend that Proverbs is a fountainhead for this moral virtue. The one who would wisely teach about sex must begin with the proverbial fundamentals.

Without blushing, Proverbs introduces the young adolescent boy to two stunning women, Lady Wisdom and Lady Folly. Lady Wisdom personifies the ecstasy to be enjoyed by the young person who chooses to embrace morality and marital fidelity. Lady Folly personifies the electrifying thrill of lust but also the shocking, burned-out end of those who choose the animal aspect of sexual desire. These two women embody two choices, one of which will lead to success in sexual relationships and the other to disaster.

The parents in Proverbs seek to entice their children to fall in love with Lady Wisdom and to see through the seductive schemes of Lady Folly. Contemporary parents must be aware of these two women and know their character thoroughly if they hope to encourage a healthy attitude toward sex in their children. Let's begin by meeting Lady Folly. What does God want His children to know about a prostitute's boudoir?

---

*Allan Bloom, *The Closing of the American Mind* (New York: Simon & Schuster, 1987).

Think About It

1. Why is it difficult for us as parents to talk to our children about sexuality? Why is it necessary for us to come to terms with our own sexual urges in order to be able to share wisely about this topic with our children?

2. On the way to get a pizza or a Big Mac with one of your teens ask them what they are learning in health class about the biological facts of sex, the danger of venereal diseases, and the most effective means to prevent infection? Don't be too quick to jump in and give your views concerning these matters. Ask questions and first discover what's going on inside your son or daughter concerning this topic. "He who answers before listening—that is his folly and shame" (18:13).

3. Make a list of the dominant sources for information concerning sex in our culture. Evaluate the truthfulness of these sources.

4. Pray together as husband and wife that you both will not be threatened by the young virility of your teens but will openly share with them biblical values about sex.

5. How would you attempt to teach a twelve-year-old about the seductive techniques of a prostitute? In the next chapter we will learn how the heavenly Father does this.

10

The Seductress

Brad is fourteen. The fuzz above his upper lip has finally thickened into whiskers, and his husky 125 pounds are spread over a five-foot seven-inch frame instead of that cursed four-foot-eleven he has been teased about for two years. He's been watching the girls with admiration since he was eleven. When a pair of long, slender legs walk by, his eyes are easily captured. But none of these desirable creatures has ever noticed him. Barbara, a seventeen-year-old senior, changes all this.

She notices Brad his first day of high school. In fact, she takes him under her wing. She sits by him at lunch. Gives him a ride home from school and invites him to parties on the weekend. "Brad, I can't believe you're only a ninth-grader. You're so mature for your age. I've never been able to open up like this with a guy. My parents never have time to listen. How could I make it without you?"

Barbara does more than talk. During breaks between classes she holds his hand. At a movie she places her hand gently on his thigh. Dropping him off at his house after school, she kisses him strongly on the lips. One afternoon she drives past Brad's street and pulls into her own driveway. The garage is empty. Both of her parents are away at work.

"Come on in for a few minutes," she invites.

Like a spark igniting gasoline, Brad's passion could become inflamed. To walk inside would mean giving to a girl who actually cared little about him what he would never again be able to give away for the first time. What could Brad's parents teach him that would help him to say no at this crucial point in his life? How could they implant in his mind the discretion to enable him to see through Barbara's flattery in the early stages of the relationship? Our kids, like Brad, will probably face Barbara's invitation. How does God prepare His children for this encounter? What does God want our kids to know about seduction and its consequences?

Proverbs responds to the sexual potency of the young by talking frankly about immorality's con game. Proverbs challenges our kids to consider what has always been true about illicit pleasure. Its teaching method uses the art of storytelling to help children imagine seduction and its consequences before they actually face it in the hallways of their middle school or high school. Proverbs 7 presents one of wisdom's dramatic presentations.

The main characters, the naive victim and the cunning huntress, walk out onto the stage of life. The parent invites his son to listen to seduction's smooth words, smell her enchanting perfume, and observe her stunning features. The teenager begins to feel the undertow of her proposition. Then at the moment of critical decision the skilled storyteller pulls the cloak of deception away and drives home the devastating consequences of falling prey to immorality's con.

Our young people daily experience this dramatic method of communicating values. The tragedy is that many movies, videos, and songs lie about the consequences of sex outside of marriage. Instead, the "party animal" becomes a hero surrounded by gorgeous women. Sitcoms assume teens who "go together" will soon go to bed together. Isolating your children will not silence these false messages. Authors and directors with strong ethical convictions need to combat this deception. We must reclaim the power of the story for good in training young men and women in our society; instead of exploiting their naiveté for material gain. Parents need to replace the perverted messages from Prince, Madonna, and Motley Crew with the valid ethics of explicit biblical narratives, such as Joseph and Potiphar's wife, Samson and Delilah, and David and Bathsheba. The Bible is hardly prudish about sex, but it is honest. Sons and daughters must hear about sex from God's perspective.

Solomon's sex education could be safely addressed to only the young men, for they would be the ones most likely to face the temptation of the street. Apparently, the daughters in the tenth century B.C. had the sense to know that sex for a woman involved much more than a few minutes of physical ecstasy. Also, the prevailing social custom of ancient Israel kept the girls at home under the loving care and protection of their fathers until the right husband could be found.

Today our daughters are exposed to the fast lane of college life or the singles scene of a large city to the same degree as our sons. Consequently, our girls, as well as our boys, need to listen to the principles taught in Proverbs, for the "mysterious woman" of Proverbs 7 is far more than a literal woman of the street. She represents all the obsession and intrigue of illicit sexuality for both males and females.

The Victim

At the window of my house
  I looked down through the lattice
and discerned among the naive a young man
  void of common sense and will.
Passing along the street near her corner
  in the evening twilight and as the dark of night set in
he took the steps which led to her house.

(7:6–9)

The entire book is an attempt to keep this young simpleton out of trouble. But as we learned in chapter one, he is headstrong and cocky. He thinks he knows more than his instructors, and his arrogant naiveté coaxes him to the wrong place at the right time. He knows where the woman lives. He knows the time of night she will be available, and he lacks the willpower to control the passion of his glands.

This is the teenager who has nothing to do on a Friday night except cruise the streets. His plan? Go out with the guys, look at the pretty girls, and boast about the one he will conquer. When Dad and Mom ask, "Where are you going tonight? What time will you be in?" He grunts and responds under his breath, "I don't know. I'm just going out with some of my friends." Adulthood to this young man means his dad and mom no longer have the right to know where he goes or what he does.

This unplanned "going out" is naive. If we allow it to occur, we are foolish. Mary is my effective ally in combating my male passivity when it comes to making our teenagers spell out their plans. Asking where they are, what they are doing, who they are with, and what time they will be in is not distrust. It is our responsibility of love. We must care enough to demand a plan. Places, activities, and times need to be nailed down so that love can make the right connections if problems arise. Life gets dangerous for kids when parents don't know where they are or who they are with, for a cat is on the prowl.

The Huntress

Now a woman comes to meet him
　dressed as a prostitute with hidden motives.
She is boisterous and rebellious.
　Her feet will not settle down in her house.
First in the street, then in the open plazas,
　finally near every corner she lurks to ambush.

(7:10–12)

The young man believes he is looking for love. The huntress knows she is hunting her game. The skillful and conscientious parent exposes the clothes and character of this female Don Juan.

Dressed as a Prostitute

She is dressed to kill. Like the Venus's flytrap, her gorgeous appearance is the captivating pull of death. This is no common street woman but a high-class number. Her carefully painted lips ooze an invitation to kiss (5:3). The flash of her eyes causes numbness to invade the young man's brain as the Novocain™ of lust dulls his senses (6:25). The legitimate wife uses the sensuousness of her lips and eyes to arouse her husband to the joys of intimacy (Song of Songs 4:1, 11), but this immoral black widow uses these feminine charms to spin her web of death. She knows that the path to a man's body begins with an assault against his eyes.

Hidden Motives

Sacred wedding vows mean nothing to the huntress. Years ago she screamed at her young husband and slammed the door of their home in his face. She abandoned this friend of her youth (2:17) to walk out into the nightlife. Now she hunts for the intoxication of sex with virgin men. These physical highs turn her life into the exhilaration of the present moment and obscure any concern regarding her destiny (4:6). Her boisterous defiance of domestic life mocks feminine gentleness and quietness (7:11). Her arrogant nonconformity causes other women to regard her with suspicion, but men find her fascinating and irresistible. They believe life with her would bring ultimate sex. Her soft skin blinds them to the granite hardness of her soul. Her words, however, (even more than her appearance) inject her most potent venom.

The Proposition

She seized him and kissed him.
 With an impudent face she said,
"I have prepared a sacrificial meal.
 Today I fulfilled my vows.
So I came to meet you,
 to look for you, and now I have finally found you.
My bed is made
 with the finest Egyptian linens.
I sprinkled it with exotic perfumes.
Come on! Let's drink our fill of sex until the morning.
 Let's enjoy love.
For the man is not at home,
 he is gone on a long trip.
He took plenty of money with him
 and won't return until the full moon." (7:13–20)

The smooth tongue of the adulteress baits the young man with three lies: It's a holiday, a time for exceptions; it's your moment to become a man; and it's your opportunity to discover the pleasure of satin sheets and reckless abandon.

The Time for Exceptions

In the ancient world the completion of a religious vow was commemorated by bringing a fellowship offering to the temple. Part of this meat was offered to the deity as a burnt offering, some was given to the priest, and the rest was eaten by the one who brought the offering that day (Leviticus 7:11–15). Special holidays were opportune times for completing such vows. Thus the temptress informs the young man that a delicious steak waits to be eaten at her table. It is their night to celebrate. An evening to remember. Everyone knows that holidays are times for exceptions.

Briefly forget the usual standards. Besides, this isn't some wicked street-walker but a good religious girl. After all, had she not been at the temple, offering sacrifices?

Our kids must be warned about the danger of the "special time," such as prom night, the night before a boyfriend or girlfriend leaves for college or reports for basic training, Mardi Gras in New Orleans, or Carnival in Rio. Immorality whispers during these times, "Ordinarily you would not do this, but this is a special moment." Our kids must also be informed that this lie can be heard not only after a heavy metal rock concert but also after a church youth group social. Religious activity is no wall against the assault of lust.

I was sitting in a seminary classroom with twenty other men studying Ephesians 4. Being immersed in parsing Greek verbs and analyzing the grammar, most of us did not note the content of Paul's warning concerning the threat of sexual impurity. "Having lost all sensitivity, they have given themselves over to sensuality so as to indulge in every kind of impurity, with a continual lust for more" (Ephesians 4:19 NIV).

One of my classmates, however, was not deaf to Paul's concern that day. Allan was a husky, masculine fellow, but his shoulders began to shake. His eyes welled with tears. "Guys, I need you all to pray for my wife and me. She's eight months pregnant, and I'm afraid something will not be right with our baby. My fear is not just due to first-baby jitters. When I was fifteen, I went to Rio during Carnival, met a knockout Brazilian, and we had relations. Just a holiday fling, but a month after I returned home I felt lousy. A doctor checked me out and gave me the news I had contracted a venereal disease.

"Later when I met Judy and we got serious about marriage, I confessed my immorality and my past infection. She forgave me, and we went ahead with the wedding. Since she became pregnant, however, I am haunted with the fear that somehow my wife and baby could suffer because of my foolishness."

Our class put the Greek parsing on hold until the next period as we devoted the rest of the hour to prayer for Judy and Allan. A month later the Lord graciously answered our prayers by giving them a healthy child.

Our heavenly Father is merciful. There was no need for Allan to fear. Penicillin had effectively cleansed his system, but his experience, even before the AIDS assault, warns us that a brief holiday fling can yield years of fear and pain. The holiday time must never become a time for making unethical exceptions.

The sequel to Allan's story warns against a more serious infection. Allan's struggle did not cease in Rio. The time for exceptions had infected him not only with a physical disease but also with a recurring moral weakness penicillin could never cure.

After graduation he became an associate pastor. I heard excellent reports about his effective ministry working with singles in a large church. About two years into the ministry, however, the report was no longer filled with blessing. Allan had to leave his ministry because he had been unfaithful to Judy.

Warning! Immorality lurks when warm brother-sister relationships generated by Christ's love give way to sexual desires ignited by Satan.

The Time to Be Macho

The huntress's sacrificial meal attempts to reach the young man's heart through his stomach. But she is far too cunning not to recognize the most direct passage to a man's heart—through his pride. "I came to meet you, to look for you, and now I have finally found you" (7:15).

Like Brad at the beginning of this chapter, a fourteen-year-old might be physically grown and filled out, yet internally he can still feel like the ten-year-old the girls laughed at or treated like their little brother. In an attempt to compensate for this poor self-image, the naive teenager often puts on macho airs. He talks sex and flirts with the girls. Many of the girls are repulsed by his behavior at first, but he soon finds that some are more than willing to fulfill his fantasies. The huntress flatters this vulnerable pride and pushes the young man into a life of consuming flames of lust.

Our sons must be warned about the smooth-tongued woman who flatters their pride, but our daughters must be warned about the "wounded puppy" who appeals to their instinct to care for the misunderstood and rejected. This is the young man who acts like the devil but confides to a beautiful young virgin that his heart is pure as gold underneath. Her motherly instincts yearn to rescue this poor boy from all the misunderstanding and hurt. Before they encounter this seduction, our daughters must be taught that they will have plenty of opportunity to mother real children if God blesses them with a family. Husbands, on the other hand, are to be respected not mothered.

The Time for Satin Sheets and Reckless Abandon

Adolescents should begin the process of learning to control the fire in their groins. Helping our teens to face sexual passion and to control it, instead of ignoring its reality, is the parents' role. The father of Proverbs 7 explains how passion is aroused through the senses. Sexy sights, exotic smells, sensuous touches rev a boy's sexual motor, and the huntress knows how to fire all the cylinders. Inside her apartment the stereo plays Ravel's *Boléro*. Her king-sized bed is turned down, and the scent of Fantasy® fills the air. She slips into something "more comfortable" and offers her young man a martini. She then invites him to come to her and drink deeply of love. This is the scene described in Proverbs 7:16–18.

Immorality consistently confuses love with lust. Passion takes the place of commitment. As the hormones surge, faithfulness, purity, truthfulness, and self-control become forgotten concepts in the moment of explosive desire. Immorality always promises, "We'll never get caught!" (7:19–20).

Richard was an executive for a Dallas computer firm. A pending contract necessitated a quick two-day trip to Los Angeles. His daughter, Deborah, was a sophomore at a large Southern California university. Arriving late, he was not able to give her a call, letting her know he was in town. While grabbing supper in the hotel restaurant, an attractive woman walked by and flipped a card on his table. When he returned to his room, he took the card from his shirt pocket.

"I've seen it on TV and in the movies. I've read about it in novels. What would it be like to have sex with another woman? Just this once! No one will ever know."

He dialed the number. In a few minutes he heard high heels clicking down the hall, followed by a gentle knock on his door. Opening the door, he gasped!

His daughter, Deborah, stood before him.

Immorality consistently promises no one will ever find out. Powerful politicians like Gary Hart, Bob Packwood, and Richard, that executive from Dallas, never imagined that their private indiscretion would be exposed and ruin their careers. For centuries the hard facts have proved that immorality has a tendency to come out of the shadows and accuse its victims in public. Dr. Bruce Waltke related this incident concerning his friend Richard while teaching a doctoral course to us on Proverbs. The last I heard, Richard was being blackmailed by his daughter, who was threatening to tell her mom about her father's attempted one-night stand. That husband, his marriage, and family need healing. We should be warned against ever listening to the seductive whisper: "It's a time for exceptions. Prove your manhood. Experience exotic pleasure. You will never get caught!"

Barbara jumps out of her car and begins to walk toward the front door. She expects Brad to follow. He opens the passenger door and gets out.

"Barb, it's 3:45. I need to get home. I've got a piano lesson tonight, and my mom will kill me if I don't get some practicing in."

The real reason Brad did not follow his girlfriend into the house? A red light had begun to flash in his head. "Danger! Beware of the time for exceptions, the time to be macho, and the time for reckless abandon. You will get caught!"

During a late-night talk with Brad while camping out together, his dad had wondered if his son was really tuned in. The incident with Barbara proved he was.

Think About It

1. Family discussion: Two young people have been dating regularly for more than a year. They believe they are in love. Would it be wise for this couple to go ahead and have sexual intercourse?

Take a careful look at 1 Thessalonians 4:3–8. Why does Paul compare sexual intercourse outside of marriage to stealing?

2. What are some examples from the movies and television where the smooth deceptive words of the immoral man or woman is presented as the truth and the kind of lifestyle to desire? What have you learned in this chapter to help counter this false advice?

11

Preventatives and Cures

Proper sex standards, not condoms, are the best preventatives against sexually transmitted diseases. But physical disease is only one of immorality's potential consequences. Straight talk about all the pain—physical, emotional, and social—that sexual sin can bring is one step we must take toward helping the next generation establish healthy sexual values.

The wise instructors in Proverbs offer far more than prophylactics to their sons. They give them the truth about the pit of sexual immorality. Illicit sex sometimes gives the thrill of a lifetime, but it is like plugging yourself into a 220-volt socket—electrifying yet deadly. We must sound the alarm! Our sons and daughters must be instructed and warned that immorality begins with an idea. Read and heed the "No Trespassing" signs. Never forget the deadly consequences. If you do fall, remember the heavenly Father offers to forgive.

Guard Your Thoughts

More than anything you protect, guard your heart, for the wellsprings of life flow from it. (4:23)

My oldest brother-in-law, John, was on vacation in Kansas City when he felt a sharp pain rather like indigestion after dinner. However, as a physician, he knew it was not from too much rich food. A trip to the emergency room and an EKG revealed that at thirty-five John was experiencing his first major heart attack. Five years and three bypass surgeries later, his body could no longer take it, and his Savior called him home. Our family experienced firsthand the importance of a healthy heart and the deadliness of a sick one. The heart is the source of physical life, and all the concern over fat and cholesterol is an attempt to guard it from disease.

Proverbs' primary concern is not with our blood pump but with the source of our moral and spiritual life. The command to "guard your heart" is not a warning to watch your cholesterol. It is a plea to guard against wrong ideas, which will clog the arteries of the soul.

Deep within our personality, wrong thinking about sex leads to sick actions in sexual relationships. At the control center of our being, thoughts and feelings generate the decisions that lead to actions, and this is where the battle begins. This is where Proverbs wants to inject the truth. This is where we must be on guard.

Our desires to satisfy sexual drives are not wrong in themselves. They are normal. The evil stems from our false belief that these desires can best be fulfilled in ways contrary to God's design and with partners He does not intend us to have. This abominable lie that we can bring love and meaning into our lives by breaking God's moral laws is the beginning of sin (Genesis 3:6). We must teach our children to recognize and detest this deception.

For men, the first assault is against the eye. A seductive glance from a forbidden woman captures his gaze. In his mind he begins to covet the experience of having intercourse with such a beauty. For many men this enslaving seduction begins with the shameless, high-gloss image of a pornographic centerfold or the high-tech wizardry of the cinema, where bigger-than-life beauties willingly shed their clothes. We must not pretend these thoughts do not invade our minds. Instead, we must decide to say no to their alluring invitation. We must correctly label them as attempts to get us to break the tenth commandment. Coveting, or lusting after, what God does not intend us to possess, is breaking the final commandment (Exodus 20:17). It is the first disobedience in sexual sin.

When a parent finds the swimsuit issue of *Sports Illustrated* underneath his twelve-year-old son's mattress, it is not the time for embarrassment and anger. The magazine needs to be trashed but without condemnation. We need to talk to him about why men drool over these photographs each winter and why he felt compelled to sneak a peek. Would his desire to look at a woman's nakedness be wrong if the woman undressing were his wife? Does he think one of these women who will take money to expose themselves to millions of men would make a dependable life partner? Could he trust her? Lust never takes the time to contemplate the truth. The truth can slash lust's grip on our minds.

Straightforward, honest discussions about sexual impulses—not denial—is necessary to protect our sons from being taken captive by the eyes of the seductress and from coveting her beauty in their hearts (6:25). Remember, it begins with an idea.

Danger! No Trespassing

Do not allow your heart to turn aside to her ways! Do not stray into her paths. (7:25)

Keep far away from her, and do not go near the door to her house. (5:8)

There are places moral people do not go and paths they do not take. In the previous chapter we learned how the huntress seduces the naive adolescent because he is at the wrong place at the right time. His parents did not set boundaries, such as requiring explicit information about what he is doing, who he is with, and what reasonable time he will be home.

Moral kids do not create fake ID cards to go nightclubbing and buy drinks. They respect themselves enough to recognize that that kind of night belongs to drunkenness and immorality. Why give your virginity away to someone you hardly know while in a state too smashed to remember?

Wise teenage couples respect the power of their sexual attraction and make a commitment not to be alone in homes or submit themselves to other situations where temptation could overwhelm them. We should discuss with our teenagers the safeguards we exercise to maintain sexual purity when, for example, we are away on a business trip. We need to discuss the kinds of doors open to them that could lead to immorality, and we can help them develop safeguards against these situations. All of us need to heed the "No Trespassing" signs.

Kids are tired of hearing adults preach about morality and proclaim, "Just say no," while watching these same adults say yes to the behaviors they warn against. Immorality is not an adolescent problem; it is a human problem, and all of us must follow the path that leads away from immorality's door. In our society it is a question of life and death.

The Deadly Consequences

Exorbitant Prices

> Lest you give the bloom of your youth to others,
>> and your years to those who are mercilessly cruel,
> lest strangers grow fat on your productivity,
>> and your sweat enriches another's house.
>
> (5:9–10)

Free love is expensive. Though many teens have no concern for the future, we need to help our kids develop this awareness. This is the purpose of Proverbs—to move naive young people living only for the present to see where their present choices will lead. Let's put a pencil to some of the costs of immorality. If a couple in high school has relations and the girl becomes pregnant who will pay the bill? Each day approximately half of the three thousand American teenage girls who find themselves in this difficulty have an abortion. Should a helpless, developing infant be forced to pay the price for someone else's passion?

Suppose the couple decides to get married and keep the baby. How will they continue their education and cover the cost of the birth? What about the baby's care? How will the young husband deal with the resentment he may feel when his peers go away to college and he is left working menial jobs to keep food on the table for his premature family? How will the young mother feel at nineteen when her girlfriends are going out on dates and she is left with a whining two-year-old not yet potty-trained?

Suppose the boy will not assume responsibility for the child. Is it right for her parents to have to pay the expenses and, as is often the case, assume the responsibility? If her parents cannot afford it, the taxpayers pay the bill for the welfare assistance. Teen couples have sex in the passion of the moment with their minds seared by the heat. Before they allow this passion to take over, they need to see the objective facts. When God's moral laws are broken, everyone in society pays.

Have we discussed with our sons what it means to "get caught with your pants down"? The extortion game is played like this: An attractive couple moves to town. The wife's provocative dress and beauty incite the men's imagination. Her husband is a workaholic. Obviously, he pays little attention to the romantic needs of his partner. She gets a job and her coworkers notice her depression. She hungers for love. Her boss's son, home from college, works in the office with her, and soon they are sharing their lunch break. After one such lunch she mentions, "I left Jack off at the airport this morning. His business will keep him away for more than a week. Why don't you come over to our place tonight and eat supper with me. I'm lonely and frightened in that big house."

The son arrives at her home and enjoys a good dinner. Her wine is exquisite, and she liberally provides refills. While watching TV, she puts her head on his shoulder. Her hand lightly touches his leg, and she kisses his neck. When his passion ignites, she pulls him to the floor.

Suddenly the darkened den blazes with light. With his pants down, the blinking young man faces her angry husband. "You are going to pay for this!" The naive young man never realized that blackmail was the game all along. This game has been played for centuries, which explains why Proverbs warns against falling into the clutches of those who are merciless and cruel.

Have our children considered that if they do not control their sexual urges before marriage, a ceremony can hardly be expected to magically give them the gift of sexual control? Promiscuity in the teen years usually doesn't disappear in the twenties. After the vows, however, the sin is adultery, not fornication.

Marital unfaithfulness is a leading cause of divorce. The maligned party often hires a merciless lawyer. The adulterer's alimony payments will enrich another's house for many years (5:10). You can never pay enough to remove the disgrace (6:32–33) or buy forgiveness from those who are hurt (6:34–35).

Our children need to be taught from their youth that immorality demands exorbitant prices. The loss of wealth is the least of the concerns. Worse is the loss of health.

Deadly Diseases

> You will groan when your end comes,
> when your body shrivels to skin and bones.
> Then you will say, "Why did I hate discipline?
> Why did my heart spurn correction?

Why wouldn't I listen to my teachers' voice?
Why wouldn't I open my ears to them?"

(5:11–12)

Why? Why? Why? The wise teachers in Proverbs knew that the dying victim of sexual immorality is perhaps the most effective sermon on the need to make an early commitment to sexual purity. The hard realities of venereal disease argue for monogamous marriages and purity in every generation, whether it be the insanity of the nineteenth-century syphilis as the brain cortex shrank slowly and relentlessly or the POW-like skeleton of the AIDS victim today, the body covered with purplish sores and the lungs starving for oxygen, but defenseless against pneumonia.

I have argued throughout this discussion that ignorance is not bliss. In some cases it could mean death. Our teenagers must know that the HIV virus is transmitted by contaminated blood in transfusions, by intravenous drug abuse, and by sexual contact with an infected member of either sex. AIDS began in the homosexual community, but it is not just a homosexual disease. Monogamous heterosexual marriage and sexual purity are the best preventatives against infection. Our children should learn these facts at home from their parents. Government pamphlets can never take the place of dads and moms. We, the parents, underestimate the influence we have on our children's lives. A health class at school cannot compete with the power of our input.

We must tell them that though 70 percent of the casualties from AIDS are homosexual and bisexual men, and 20 percent are intravenous drug uses, 4.3 percent are heterosexuals whose only risk factor was that they had intimate sexual contact with an infected partner. Surgeon General Koop wrote out his most effective prescription: abstinence before marriage and sex within a monogamous marriage. I would argue that condoms are a poor, uncertain alternative for those who refuse to commit themselves to purity; they are better than no protection, yet hardly foolproof. Their effectiveness against AIDS isn't any better than their effectiveness as a birth control method.

Our children should have the same fear of immorality they would have of an archer poised to drill their gut with a hunting arrow (7:23). When tempted to indulge my illicit sexual appetites, I find the thought of an arrow protruding from my liver an effective deterrent.

As in Russian roulette, some play the game and apparently escape the consequences. The immoral individual fails to remember, however, that his or her private indiscretions could become public scandal any day.

Ruined Reputations

I have come to the brink of complete ruin in the midst of the public hearings of the society. (5:14)

Whether indecent exposure occurs on Capitol Hill with a powerful congressman, or in the pulpit with a revered clergyman, sexual sin costs you your reputation. Our society plays a dirty game. Novels, movies, and television communicate the image that everyone sleeps around at times. James Bond and even the nineties version of Batman fight never-ending battles against evil and injustice; but going to bed with beautiful women outside of marriage is not considered to be part of the evil. Yet when individuals are entrusted with responsibility in real-life society, suddenly adultery, liaisons with prostitutes, and even having to get married in your youth becomes a blot against your character. If a person commits treason against his or her wedding vows, how can our nation be secure in such hands?

Political candidates whine about the prudery of the idealistic right and portray themselves as victims of media sensationalism.

But even if they deliberately ignore the Judeo-Christian ethics presented in Proverbs that our nation was founded upon, they could read the identical advice in the writings of Ani, an Egyptian wise man who wrote to men aspiring for government positions. Much of this advice is simply common sense known for centuries.

> Be on your guard against a woman from abroad, whom no one knows in her city. Do not gaze at her when she goes past, and do not know her carnally. She is deep water, the extent of which no one knows. A woman whose husband is far away says daily to you, "I am polished [pretty]!" when she has no witnesses. She waits and sets her trap. A great crime—and death, when it is known.*

The Internet generation may think they can change the rules. Yet for thousands of years, men and women who are loose sexually lose their political positions and power. Wise parents expose the nakedness of the media hype and teach their children moral standards that will make them credible candidates in every generation.

Forgiveness for the Fallen

Proverbs trains our children in the school of skillful living. Moral purity is the standard that protects them from ruined wealth, health, and reputation. This principle is life-saving, but what about those already drowning in immorality? Is there hope for the fallen?

Our children should learn the facts of sin in our homes, but they should also experience the warmth of forgiveness. James, a New Testament teacher in the tradition of Proverbs, unmasked immorality as the greedy passion for selfish pleasure (James 4:3–4). All sin is "adultery" against God and makes Him an enemy far more dangerous than a maligned partner in a marital suit. Yet He is not a merciless, cruel enemy. He offers grace to those who humbly admit their treachery and return to nearness with Him (Proverbs 3:34, James 4:6–8). Those who genuinely grieve over the personal hurt they have brought God and to others experience God's gentle hands lifting them up to renewed purity. Jesus, the faithful Son, took the punishment. There is nothing left to do but admit sin and ask our heavenly Father to forgive us. He never fails to restore His children to intimacy (1 John 1:9). A stress upon the holy standards of the Judeo-Christian ethic without this acceptance of God's forgiving grace provided in His Son generates a rigid moralism and hypocrisy impotent to restrain illicit sexual drives.

Satan's most cunning lie about sexual sin is that it is unforgivable. The words from the victim sound so pious: "My case is hopeless. The dirt is too ingrained for even God to clean." But this is a lie, a deception to be resisted (James 4:7). This is not humility but an arrogant refusal to accept God's truth about restoration. Hopelessness becomes the excuse for continued addiction to immorality. "God mocks the proud, but gives gracious forgiveness to the humble" (Proverbs 3:34, James 4:10).

Mick, a young Christian truck driver barreled his eighteen-wheeler down the night highway. Adultery had taken him captive during the past weeks. The lust for exotic sexual thrill, titillated by the raw pornography at truck stops, had driven him out of an eight-year marriage into a drunken, drug-filled world of illicit sex. Sessions with a Christian counselor could not penetrate the haze of immoral deceit. His believing wife slept alone while he gave his lust to a whore.

That night the eighteen-wheeler's cassette player cried out into the fog. "Are you living in an old man's rubble? Are you listening to the father of lies? If you are, then you're headed for trouble. If you listen too long you'll eventually die." The powerful words of Amy Grant's music deeply rebuked Mick's heart. Where a counselor's verbal communication could not reach, the Holy Spirit's music pierced evil's armament. Mick began to return to faithfulness and purity.

Today, after much prayer and counsel, Mick is one with his Lord and with his wife. He is a believer in the proverbial preventatives as he teaches these safeguards to the precious daughter God gave to him and his wife when he returned home. Use God's preventatives, and remember there is forgiveness and restoration for the guilty. "If we confess our sins, he is faithful and just and will forgive us our sins and purify us from all unrighteousness" (1 John 1:9 NIV).

* Walter Beyerlin, *Near Eastern Religious Texts Relating to the Old Testament* (Philadelphia: Westminster, 1978, p. 48).

Think About It

1. I presented *Sports Illustrated's* annual swimsuit issue as one illustration of the attack Satan makes against our eyes. What are some other illustrations? What steps are you taking with your family to insure that the truth about sexual desire is communicated and is lived?

2. How do you discern the difference between a legitimate desire and a false desire? Try to have a discussion with your son or daughter about how you resist illicit sexual desires. If your teenage years or adult years were not marked by sexual purity, don't allow the guilt to keep you from giving instruction about this area. First John 1:9 states that Jesus Christ can forgive our sins, and King David, after committing adultery with Bathsheba, taught others how to escape the sex sin that ensnared him. (Note Psalm 51:12–13.)

3. Family discussion: In this chapter we discussed many of the deadly consequences resulting from sexual sin. Read back over these consequences and then have your family share about how these conse-

quences are often ignored in our society. (An example would be the presentation of Magic Johnson as a hero after he went public about being HIV positive, the virus that causes AIDS. The media's failure to admit that his promiscuous behavior was the reason he contracted the disease is wrong.)

4. Is sexual sin unforgivable? Is Jesus' sacrifice on Calvary powerful enough to cleanse an immoral heart? Then why do many young people and adults who have fallen in this area feel second rate in God's family? What are some steps we can take to defeat this illegitimate guilt?

12

The Intoxicating Wife

Gary and Susan settled into their seats and fastened their safety belts. The pace of the frantic day—pictures at 12:30, the wedding ceremony at 2:00, the reception line from 2:45–3:30, the dash to the best man's car, and the procession of honking to the Austin airport, checking baggage, boarding the jet—finally eased. The newlyweds could settle back for three hours and try to relax.

"This is the best airline steak I ever had. Even this artificial cake tastes like Mom's, fresh out of the oven." Gary tried to make small talk with Susan. His stomach remembered he had not eaten since the rehearsal dinner the night before. He watched Susan struggle to keep her eyes open as exhaustion rocked her to sleep. *I can't believe it! Our marriage is only two hours old, and already I've put my wife to sleep.* As Gary finished his tray, the thought of going to bed dominated his thought, and sleep was the last thing he wanted.

The mountains blocked the sun in the west, shooting spectacular reds, oranges, and yellows into the sunset as their flight circled Denver's airport. It seemed to take forever to reclaim their luggage but only moments to claim a brand-new rental car. They drove an hour west into the privacy of the mountains.

The lodge was nestled among the Aspens. In December, skiers would crowd to grab a room this close to the slopes. Yet in early June, only a few vacationers were in the lobby as the newlyweds registered and retired to their room.

"Gary, go ahead and use the bathroom first, I'll unpack our things." Susan tried to quiet her nerves by placing their clothes in the drawers. In less than two minutes Gary's teeth were brushed, and he made his reentry into their room dressed in the brand-new, white, silk pajamas his mom commanded him to wear.

"Your turn, Honey."

It doesn't take a man long to take care of things before he goes to bed, Susan thought as she disappeared into the bathroom with a small suitcase. Gary waited.

Alone in the bathroom Susan was petrified. Since puberty her dad had warned her about immorality. When her friends in high school boasted of their prowess in bed, she braced herself against the peer pressure and guarded her virginity. When she and Gary began going together, they carefully controlled the physical side of their relationship. Susan appreciated Gary's patience, and his self-control won her trust. Both decided to save intercourse for their wedding night. The night was now here.

Susan loved Gary. She knew the biological mechanics of intercourse, but as her satin skin became rough with goose bumps, the wedding night jitters became dark fears.

Susan's parents had done an excellent job warning her against the pit of sexual immorality, but they had not spoken freely to her about the fountain of marital sexual love. They, like many parents, believed that telling teenagers too much about the joys of sex in marriage would entice them to eat the fruit too soon. The result: Susan knew in her mind that God smiled upon sex in marriage, but her emotions still screamed, "It's dirty and ugly!"

How can we warn our kids against the deadly consequences of immorality without causing their emotions to become frigid?

We have listened as the parents in Proverbs warn against the deadly consequences of sexual sin. Christian teens constantly hear these words of warning. Do we share with them equally about the positive side of sex? Proverbs 5:15–23 stops sounding the dreadful alarms and goes on to ring the bells of celebration. The Creator wants His kids to relish the intoxicating pleasure of making love in marriage. The Bible is pure, but never prudish, about sex.

The Exclusive Fountain

> Drink water from your own cistern,
>> flowing water from your own well.
> Why should your springs overflow in the street,
>> channels of water in the public squares?
> Let them be for yourself alone,
>> never shared with strangers.
> Let your fountain be blessed,
>> and rejoice in the wife of your youth.
>
> (5:15–17)

In a culture where an ice-cold drink is just a refrigerator away, with the choice of cubed or crushed ice, the priceless prize of a private garden fountain is not appreciated. In the arid regions of ancient Palestine, men killed for exclusive rights to a well. The wise Israelite father compared this cherished pleasure of a drink to the refreshing pleasures of monogamous sex. We could paraphrase his thought like this: "Son, making love in marriage is the coolness of Rocky Mountain spring water on parched lips when the temperature soars over 100 degrees. Drink only from your private, unpolluted source!" (cf. Song of Solomon 4:15).

After commending sexual refreshment in marriage, the father contrasts the ugliness of taking this exclusive pleasure and making it cheap by having sex with multiple partners. Sex is too exquisite to share with someone you happened to meet at a party or on the street. The father in Proverbs compares casual sex to the wastefulness of throwing sparkling spring water into the gutter. The threat of AIDS sends a similar cold chill through our modern swinging singles scene.

Observe the dirty graffiti used for sex in the marketplace, and you will see how, when open lust replaces exclusive devotion, the purity of sex becomes more filthy than slush on a New York City street in winter.

God's special gift issuing from the pleasures of marital love are the children conceived in this union (5:18, cf. Psalm 127:3–5). Immorality breeds homeless, uncared-for street orphans (5:16). Exclusive marital intercourse gives birth to cherished kids with a dad and mom to help them learn to live. From Asian-American children in the streets of Saigon to the corpses of aborted babies at U.S. clinics, immorality is always the enemy of children.

The Exhilarating Pleasure

Rejoice in the wife of your youth!
A lovely doe, a graceful deer—
    be intoxicated with her breasts always,
    be drunk continually with her sensuous love-making.
Why go astray and get drunk sexually with a stranger?
    Why would you ever embrace the chest of a
    treacherous immoral woman?

                       (5:18–20)

Obviously this father knows the intense, satisfying high of intercourse with the one woman who has promised to make love only with him. He teaches his son the truth about where the lasting sexual highs can be found. This father shares the romantic secret of using caressing words before caressing with his hands in love. Not uptight about talking about sex with his son, the poet in him expresses himself. He compares a young wife's physical grace and beauty to the gentle sensuousness of a young doe.

Without turning red he speaks to his son about the intoxication a wife's breasts can give to her husband. If the stuffy Victorian objects to speaking with teenagers about the sexual thrill a woman's and a man's body can bring in a marriage, he or she should know that the original Hebrew text is more erotically explicit than I have been in my translation.

In chapter 14 we will devote an entire chapter to warnings about alcoholic intoxication, but here let's examine how sexual intoxication with your wife is a divine imperative (cf. 1 Corinthians 7:2–5). The intense ecstasy of marital intercourse is the only divinely applauded inebriation I know of in Scripture. When it comes to frank discussions with our young people about the thrills of sex in marriage, our prudishness will not keep them from discovering the details of intercourse. It simply guarantees that they often learn these facts from the serpent's sources—locker rooms, novels, movies, and supposedly "amoral" discussions in health class. This perpetuates Satan's lie that God is the scrooge of sexual pleasure. "Love God and become celibate, or reject Him and fulfill your sexual dreams." Godly parents attack this lie with the truth about sex from Proverbs. We should read and discuss Song of Solomon, God's celebration of marital intercourse, with our teenagers. We must resist the Christian culture's history of asceticism toward sex. If we believe in the authority of the Bible above religious prudery, we should not be afraid to expose our children to God's thoughts in His Word about the erotic intoxication of marital sex.

The Sacred Meaning

For this reason a man will leave his father and mother and be joined to his wife, and the two will become one flesh. (Genesis 2:24)

This is a profound mystery—but I am talking about Christ and the church. (Ephesians 5:32)

God would hardly take something dirty and ugly and use it as His artistic masterpiece to depict physically the intense intimacy and devotion enjoyed by Christ and His bride. Priceless works of art are honored in guarded, exclusive museums; they are not passed around on the street. The sacredness of sex as an object lesson of the oneness believers enjoy with Christ must be guarded in the hallowed halls of marriage. This explains God's hatred of promiscuity and His satisfaction with His children's lovemaking in marriage. The author of Hebrews summarized the heavenly Father's sexual views: "Marriage is to be prized and honored always, and marital intercourse considered pure. This value God places on marital love explains why He judges fornicators and adulterers" (Hebrews 13:4).

Susan does not need to despair because of her goose bumps as she faces a new experience. She can be certain she is doing nothing wrong. Her heavenly Dad will be pleased when she joins with her husband. Gary and Susan do not need to be embarrassed about their fumbling tries as they begin to learn the art of love. They have a lifetime to learn how to drink deeply of the pleasures. If, in the depths of their personalities, they grow confident that God smiles upon their physical union, they will discover their private, exclusive style for celebrating oneness in reflection of the unity they enjoy with their Savior. This is not cold theology but the reason why marital sexuality is such a celebration in heaven and on earth. "They were both naked, the man and his wife, and they were unashamed" (Genesis 2:25).*

* For further discussion of the biblical meaning of sexuality see my book *Love Without Shame: Sexuality in Biblical Perspective* (Grand Rapids, Discovery House Publishers, 1991).

Think About It

1. Beginning in the second century and enduring throughout history, the view of sex as evil in itself has been promoted by the Christian church. For example, the idea of celibacy for priests who wanted to devote themselves to the service of God came from the notion that they would be more holy if they abstained from sexual intercourse.

Read 1 Corinthians 7:9. What was the apostle Paul's practical advice to young people who found themselves in love and intensely desiring to have sex with one another? Read 1 Timothy 4:1–3. How does false religion seek to rob us of legitimate pleasure in the name of "holiness"? Does this restrictive spirit help us to resist illegitimate passion?

2. Read back over the paraphrase of Proverbs 5:18–20 on page 162. How does this open celebration of the joys of marital love make you feel? Do you think it is a good idea for our teenagers to know that God intended and looks with favor upon the joys of marital intercourse? What are some ways that you can help your children to know that God hates sexual sin because it spoils the joys of marital sex? Pray that the Lord will help you and your children to follow His balanced instruction in this area.

3. What do you think a dad and mom should communicate to their son or daughter before their wedding night about sexual intercourse? It might be wise to go down to a Christian book store and look over some of the material written on the act of marriage from a biblical perspective. *Intended for Pleasure* by Dr. Ed Wheat would be an excellent resource.

13

God's Liberated Woman

Something rare and beautiful is deemed priceless. In our liberated society you can find effective women executives, doctors, lawyers, astronauts, judges, and politicians. A few years ago, finding women in such professions was rare, but if you interviewed the women on college campuses across the United States today regarding their career choices, you would recognize that these kinds of achievements for women will probably cease to be the exception.

Mention the "biblical view of women" to some career-minded feminists and they picture silent slaves, barefoot and pregnant, locked inside their houses, forced to meet the needs of overbearing, chauvinistic husbands. They react to this traditional view with enthusiastic cheers for the woman who escapes from the drudgery of dusting, vacuuming, and wiping runny noses to the power, money, and travel of a career. Their hero is the woman who never spoiled her figure by giving birth to a child. They forget to mention she spends Mother's Day in a high-class club with a couple of other divorcees and no family.

The Adversary's distortions of the Architect's designs amaze me. He always pushes things to extremes, causing us to miss the Creator's intent. Proverbs attacks both male chauvinism and radical feminism. While it hardly expects women to lock themselves in their homes because of some inherent vulnerability, neither does it view them as Venus's flytraps, agents of seduction and death.

What qualities does our heavenly Father cherish in a woman? These are the fashions our daughters need to allow God to develop in their lives. These are the qualities our sons need to look for in a lifelong ally. A competent, godly wife was rare three thousand years ago. Solomon could not find one, though he tried a thousand times (Ecclesiastes 7:28), which says more about his character than about women in general. Such a woman is still rare today. When found, this gem is far more than an intoxicating playmate in bed. She is a priceless gift from the Lord—the personification of wisdom herself. "A home and wealth can be inherited from fathers or grandfathers, but a wife who acts with reason, forethought, and self-control is a gift received only from the LORD" (Proverbs 19:14).

Confident Trust

> Who can find a noble wife?
>   Her value far exceeds the cost of diamonds!
> Her husband trusts her deeply in his heart,
>   and he never lacks valuables.
> She does him good, not harm,
>   all the days of her life.
>
> (31:10–12)

The designation "noble wife" should forever silence the charge of chauvinism against the Bible. Women are never treated as inferior, weak, second-class. The phrase used to describe the wife of Proverbs 31 literally means "a woman of strength, might, and power." It describes King David's mighty warriors (2 Samuel 23:20, 24:2) and God's prowess over His enemies (Psalm 59:11). The gutsy widow, Ruth, who chose to leave her homeland and carve out an existence with her aged mother-in-law in a foreign land, was referred to as a "noble woman" by Boaz, the man who made her both his wife and the grandmother of King David (Ruth 3:11). This coveted title describes a woman admired by all for her industry, discipline, and moral fiber. Dependability is the heart of her durable nobility.

Unlike the seductress, this woman remains faithful to her sacred marriage vows (2:16–17). She imitates her God by keeping her promises. She does not enter marriage for experimental purposes but for keeps. "Till death do us part" is not an anachronism in her ceremony. Consequently, her husband never doubts her commitment to him. Truthfulness is at the core of her personality, and a woman of integrity never plays around behind her husband's back. As Joseph communicated to Potiphar's wife, our sons and daughters need to view infidelity as a treasonous breech of trust and a relationship to be feared. But a son can trust his life to a valiant wife of integrity.

After more than thirty years of marriage, I admire my Mary's truthful dependability more than ever. When we first started dating in the summer of 1968 I knew immediately that this woman told it like it was; her lips were connected to her heart.

We had dated a couple of weeks near the end of the camping season. On our day off I invited her to a family picnic. After lunch we were sitting on a rock alone in the middle of an Adirondack Mountain stream. Mary turned away from the small talk and said directly, "Dave, is this only a summer romance for you, or does it mean something more? My heart is beginning to respond. If you're just having a good time at the end of camp, I want to know!"

Mary's frank integrity forced me to come to grips with my own feelings. The next spring I asked her to marry me and gave her a diamond. We have now enjoyed over two dozen summers together as husband and wife, and I still treasure her straightforward honesty; trust is the foundation of a marriage.

When someone tells the truth, you can put your confidence in him or her. The wise father and mother of Proverbs warn us never to trust in money (11:28) or self-sufficiency (28:26). Repeatedly they exhort us instead to "trust in the LORD with all of our heart" (3:5, 16:20, 28:25, 29:25). When a man leans on the Lord and the Lord gives him the gift of a godly wife, Proverbs then urges him to put confidence in her and her abilities (31:11).

Biblical leadership never browbeats others into submission. It creates an environment of support and encouragement so that others blossom into all that God desires them to be. His wife's talents do not intimidate the godly husband. When he discovers her special skills, he builds her confidence and praises her effectiveness. As a result he enjoys the dividends from this investment in her competence.

Competent Household Management

The Apparel Mart

> She carefully searches for the right raw materials—
>> wool and flax,
>> and then creatively works with her hands with
>> pleasure . . .
> She holds the wool or flax distaff in her hand,
>> and her fingers grasp the spindle . . .
> When snow falls she is not worried about her family,
>> they are all clothed in warm scarlet wool. . . .
> For her beds she makes beautiful spreads.
>> Her garments are fashioned in fine Egyptian linen
>> and Tyrian purple.
>
>> (31:13, 19, 21–22)

Thumbing through McCall's®, Butterick®, and Simplicity® patterns, pawing through piles of material, finding the right thread and buttons—this was a foreign world to me before marriage. No longer! Mary's sewing ability was hardly on my list of qualifications for a wife, but her expert skills put sports jackets on my back in seminary and clothes on her children as our household grew. When I was a bachelor, clothes were not on my priority list, but now I realize they are a strategic necessity. Mary's sharp eye for sales can also dress her household in style.

Proverbs 31 portrays the noble wife as an astute buyer of material (31:13), a creative designer (31:13), a dexterous spinner of the thread (31:19), and an expert tailor (31:21). Before anyone demeans these tasks as "women's work," remember that textiles, fashion design, manufacturing, and the marketing of apparel are big business. Manhattan reserves an entire district for the garment industry.

Household furnishing was another one of those areas that hardly affected my life as a single. Who cared what was thrown over my blankets and sheets, or what material was hung around a window? Marriage opened my eyes to a miracle—even a cheap apartment could be transformed into a home by the touch of a skillful wife. Curtains and quilts make an incredible change in decor.

When Mary asked Nonnie Lewis in our church to teach her to quilt, I did not realize this would transform the simple task of going to bed at night into a tactical nightmare. The only place we had room to set up the quilting frame was directly over our bed. Each night she instructed me how to help her move the contraption up against the wall. Each night I questioned the worth of the sewing clique's spending hours talking and doing handwork on a spread-cover. A trip to Lancaster County, Pennsylvania, changed my mind.

Lancaster is the capital city of quilting, and as Mary took me from one store to the next she inquired about every new design and material combination. I asked about the prices. When we returned home I approached Mary with an idea. "Honey, we have quilts on our beds, by our stove, and in the closet. Let's sell some of them. They're a gold mine." She did not respond favorably, but I have never demeaned the expertise involved in sewing little scraps of material together in intricate patterns to make a work of art so practical it keeps you warm in the cold of winter. Our heavenly Father is concerned not only about the quilts on our beds but also the threads on our backs.

God's daughters should dress for Him. This does not require gunny sacks and combat boots. He does get furious when His daughters forget the needs of the poor and live for extravagant clothes, jewelry, and perfume (Isaiah 4:16–24). He encourages a woman to enhance her beauty with tasteful dress. The noble wife wore dresses made of the finest materials. We are responsible to help our daughters be modest, not dowdy.

A little girl asked her grandmother, "Could you show me how to sew like you?" A young wife went to an elderly Texas woman and asked, "Could you teach me to quilt?" I thank the Lord that these skills were passed on from the last generation to my wife. I do not resent expert female surgeons, lawyers, and bank presidents. Yet I am concerned. In a society of day-care centers, career worries, and mortgage payments, who will have the time to teach the household arts to the next generation of little girls?

The Culinary Specialist

> She can be compared to the shrewd merchant with ships
> > laden with valuable goods;
> > she brings her groceries from a distance.
> She gets up before dawn
> > and begins to prepare meals for her family
> > and assign the duties of her household attendants.

(31:14–15)

When I go to the grocery store for an item, I pick the one nearest to me, rush through the express line, and head for home. Mary searches the newspaper for coupons, reaches to the back of the shelf for the cans stamped with cheaper prices, and drives from one store to the next to catch all the bargains. The Phoenician merchants were the cunning buyers of the ancient world. The shrewd purchasing skills of a diligent American housewife would have given them stiff competition.

Food is another basic necessity. The wife who saves on the grocery bill and still feeds her family in style deserves all the praise we can give. The profession of housewife is not for couch potatoes (31:15, 18, 27). Before dawn she must hit the floor running to get lunches prepared and send the children to school. In the evening she must still have the energy to pat backs and sing softly as her children fade into sleep.

God's plan for our daughters may not include a husband and children. He has special responsibilities for singles. But all of our daughters and sons need to be raised to stand up and cheer for moms on Mother's Day. Effective management in a boardroom is nice, but effective management in a household is vital to all of our security.

Competent Business Expertise

Textiles

> She makes lightweight linen garments, and sells them.
> She also wholesales fine sashes to the Phoenician traders.
> (31:24)

We have already admired her family's attire. Her weaving and sewing skills do not end, however, with putting clothes on her family. She converts her talents into profits. She persists in bartering with the wily traders of her day, and, as a result, the profits for her textile and clothing businesses are so strong she decides to enter the real estate market.

Real Estate and Viticulture

> After careful consideration of a field, she buys it.
> From the profit of her sewing enterprises she plants a
>   vineyard.
> She hikes up her dress and gets down to business.
> She tastes the sweetness of harvest.
> Urged on by success she works late into the night.
>
> (31:16–18)

Hardly the cowed housewife, this woman confidently evaluates the real estate market and uncovers an investment opportunity. With her textile and clothing profits she invests in a field. After the transaction, she executes her plan and develops a vineyard, a major source of revenue in ancient Israel. Her daily workouts provide the physical strength she needs to cultivate and plant her vines (31:17, 25). Her confidence grows with each successful marketing of her crop. This hardly fits the caricature of the biblical housewife today, too afraid to sign her own checks or venture out into the public domain. The wise husband will learn not to be insecure about his wife's successes.

Catherine's son and daughter were entering high school, and the family budget was squeezed. A few dollars for college could certainly help. An opportunity at a local real estate agency presented itself. A devoted housewife, Catherine debated going out into the business world. "My days of changing diapers and watching *Sesame Street* with toddlers has slipped past," she reasoned. "John and Cathy are not helpless. If something comes up at school during the day—I'll make it clear from the beginning to my employers—I will leave, no matter what, and tend to my kids." Wondering if anyone would hire a woman with these priorities and stipulations, she interviewed for the job.

Catherine did more than get the position—she won major sales awards. She had a special knack for discerning the buyer's needs and fitting houses with these desires. She did leave the office when her teenagers needed her during the day and came home when they got out of school. When her nest emptied, the adjustment was easier. Already she and her husband had begun to move to a new page of their lives. They now had enough money in the bank to take some of those trips they had dreamed about.

A young mother of four children who are all under the age of seven must not read Proverbs 31 as a list of her day's required activities. After reading the above example about Catherine, she should not decide to go out and sell houses. She needs to read this section of Proverbs as an ideal sketch of a lifetime—a video documenting years, not a snapshot of a moment. Remember, the Proverbs 31 woman has adult children with families of their own (31:28). Our daughters must recognize there is a time for everything; no need to cram a lifetime into a day. Let's help them think through the progressive stages of life and enjoy the unique opportunities at every step. This will protect them from Wonder Woman Burnout.

Godly Instruction and Modeling

With an open hand she gets involved and aids those
   bowed down in affliction.
She reaches with both hands to those needing help . . .
When she opens her mouth, she speaks wisdom.
Her tongue forms kind, dependable instruction.

(31:20, 26)

Though not a self-indulgent yuppie, this woman does have upward mobility. However, her eyes see past her own selfishness to the crying needs of the suffering. Those in the hospital can count on her visit. Those wiping away tears of grief can count on her for a warm meal. She never forgets to send peanut butter that the missionary cannot purchase for his or her kids, remembering that Peter Pan® is hard to find in the jungle. Some of my greatest encouragements to continue to follow Christ has come from the unexpected gifts of love that godly women have extended. From the godly mom of Proverbs 31 to Dorcas of Joppa in Acts 9, God always extols the unselfish woman who fills her days with acts of kindness and love toward others. Hollywood will not produce a sitcom about her, but Jesus will praise her before His throne.

Quietness, not silence, is a virtue in a woman. The movie *Yentl* debated a woman's right to read the Torah and study theology. Proverbs presents a woman who not only learned Torah, but also teaches others (31:26). Together with her husband she warns her children against the dangers of illicit wealth and sex (1:8 ff., 6:20 ff.). The teaching of King Lemuel's mother about immorality and alcoholism (31:3–4), and the need for social justice (31:5–9) was so powerful that God chose to include it in His inspired writings. This mother's instruction on drinking will provide the basis of our discussion in the next chapter.

The godly wife is submissive to her husband and works for his good (31:12, 23; cf. Ephesians 5:21–24), but she is not inferior. She banks on family-enhancement, not self-enhancement. As life matures, what interest does her investment yield?

Applause from God, Family, and Friends

Her sons get up and bless her;
   her husband joins them, and sings her praises,
'Many women have lived nobly,

but you have excelled higher than all of them.'
A charming personality is deceptive and breathtaking
beauty a vapor,
but the woman who reverences the Lord, she is to be
praised!
Give her the fruit of her hands;
in the gates of the city honor her for her accomplishments.

(31:28–31)

The message is ancient, but our sons still need to hear it. Like the writer of Proverbs, Charles Dickens astutely penetrated human nature. Young David Copperfields are forever blinded by the flighty charm and beauty of delicate Doras. They overlook their undependableness and dream of the ecstasy of making love to such a creature. Their eyes are too immature to see the competent, quiet beauty of the sisterly Agnes. Proverbs 31 counsels that the Agneses, not the Doras, make the best wives. The most important quality in any woman is her commitment to the foundation of a skillful life—a reverential relationship with God.

The 1290 score on her SAT won Nanette a National Merit Scholarship and the right to go to the university of her choice with all expenses paid. The pre-med department of Baylor University opened its arms to this young woman with the brain power to maintain better than a 3.9 grade point average over four years. While studying biology and chemistry at Baylor, Nanette met another pre-med student only one year ahead of her.

Bob was her match in studies, and, instead of competing, they decided to join forces. A few weeks after Nanette's graduation from Baylor they married, and she joined Bob in attending the University of Texas Medical School at Galveston. With Bob in his second year and Nanette in her first, they faced the grind together.

Their mutual encouragement and support helped both to excel. During Nanette's second year they began to look forward to a lot more than their graduation from medical school. Their first child was due in November.

About four months before the delivery, Nanette was reading Philippians 2:3–4: "Do nothing out of selfish ambition or vain conceit, but in humility consider others better than yourselves. Each of you should look not only to your own interests, but also to the interests of others" (NIV). The Holy Spirit challenged her to evaluate her personal reasons for wanting to be a doctor. *Approval by others or concern for others? Recognition or a desire to heal the sick? Money or ministry?* Bob gave Nanette the space to work through the decision herself.

After finishing her exams, she decided that the hectic frenzy of juggling classes, labs, and tests, with diapers, bottles, and baby-sitters, was not the Lord's will for her. Nanette dropped out of med school and committed herself to the full-time profession of being a wife and raising small children. Bob and Nanette now enjoy not one, but two children.

When I called her on the phone I could hear both kids crying for Mommy. "Nanette, don't you think you should reconsider and return to your medical training?"

She laughed, "Dave, I've never regretted my decision. I have time to read my Bible and pray. I can give a sympathetic ear to friends who need to talk on the phone. I have time to give myself to needs at church. I can give myself to Bob and the kids. There is one thing I am tired of hearing—the reaction I get from the contemporary society, 'How could you ever give up a medical career to be only a housewife!' "

Now in her late twenties, Nanette most likely will have time later to invest her talents in endeavors outside her home, but for now, in spite of society's ridicule, I know two small children who are glad Mom decided to stay home. I believe they will grow up and sing her praises.

Our homes and churches need to be places where wives and mothers are adored, praised, and applauded.

Think About It

1. In Proverbs 31:10–12 the writer expresses the importance of being able to put confident trust in one's wife. Why is trust so imperative in any relationship? Why is it so important in the marriage relationship? How is one's "trustability" earned?

2. Family discussion: Girls now play competitive sports, join police forces, and often earn law and medical degrees. What do you think about the change in women's role in our society? Evaluate these changes based upon what you have learned together in this chapter about characteristics of the woman described in Proverbs 31.

3. Read back over Nanette's story on pages 177–178. Do you think she made the correct choice not to finish medical school? Why or why not?

4. Think of some ways today that the wife and mother in your home can be praised. Now go ahead and express this.

Leadership Blueprints

Separate from intoxication, immorality, and injustice;
get involved and assert godly leadership in the community.

14

The Spiked Punch Bowl

Newly elected President Bill Clinton called his inaugural celebration "democracy's big day." Brent Stephens, a freshman representative, agreed with the president, but for that country-boy-turned-congressman, the celebration lasted longer than inauguration day.

Still awed by his seat in the House of Representatives, he felt he must oblige the nonstop evening reception circuit. Though drained financially by his wife's designer dresses, and emotionally by the push to complete his party's Contract with America, Brent dressed for yet another Saturday gala.

The 8:00 p.m. classical concert at the Kennedy Center had satisfied his soul. By 10:00 his stomach urged him to satisfy his hunger. Across the ballroom his wife struggled to waltz with one of the portly Washington elites. Before rescuing her, Brent decided to sample the serving tables smothered in fine cuisine and silver punch bowls—two large urns with Greek goddesses spouting continuous streams of refreshment from their mouths.

"How do you know which bowl to get a drink from?" Brent was glad the senior senator from New York was also visiting the table. Protocol was strategic in Washington, and he did not intend to prove himself an idiot in his first months on the job. "Son, it depends upon what you mean by drink. Do you happen to remember John Tower of Texas from the George Bush era? He was a powerful senator, and the president nominated him for

Secretary of Defense. Congressional hearings, however, publicized a serious a problem with alcohol. He was not confirmed. Since the Tower debacle, this bowl here is for young Congressmen who aspire to higher office. This spiked one is for those without such aspirations."

The irony of this joke is that when John Tower came to Washington, few believed too much alcohol at a Washington party could cost a man his career. Such modern ignorance is inexcusable. Three thousand years ago King Lemuel's mother warned her son about the danger of mixing drinks with government service. Throughout history, the lure of wine, like that of immoral women, has ruined political careers. Our children need to be warned about the drug that costs our society more than $117 billion a year "in everything from medical bills to lost workdays," and more deaths than AIDS, heroin, cocaine, marijuana, and crack combined (Loran Archer, deputy director of National Institute on Alcohol Abuse and Alcoholism, *Time*, November 30, 1987, p. 81).

Controlled by the Spirits

Mom's Inspired Counsel

> The words of King Lemuel, an inspired correction, which his mother taught him. 'What, my son, what can I say to prepare you for rule; the son I carried for nine months, the son I prayed for?
>
> (31:1–2)

Like the wise mother in Proverbs 4:3, Lemuel's mom knows how to express her tender affection for her son. She remembers how she cherished the developing baby in her womb. She reminds him often how he came as an answer to her prayers. How different from some mothers who shred their children's sense of value by talking about their conception as a bad accident. We are reminded again that effective parental instruction begins in the womb of intimacy. Lemuel's mom wrestles with the need to prepare him for his position of power, and God chose to inspire the straightforward advice she gave.

The Intoxication-Injustice Connection

> Do not give away your virility to immoral women,
> your career to those who destroy kings.
> It is not right for kings, Lemuel—
> it is not right for kings to drink wine,
> or for rulers to ask, "Where are the hard drinks?";
> lest they drink and forget what is decreed by law
> and twist the courts decision against all the children
> of oppression . . .
> Open your mouth for those unable to speak for themselves,
> and defend the rights of all those who are deprived.
> Open your mouth; render a just decision;
> plead the cause of the poor and the needy.
>
> (31:3–5, 8–9)

Intoxication, like immorality, perverts justice. Exposed candidates cry out against the *injustice* of evaluating their fitness for public office on the basis of their conduct in private life. Lemuel's mother had the common sense to know that when a judge drank too much and slept around with women, he would never muster the moral fortitude to stand up for a Black or Hispanic unjustly accused of stealing by the big business landlord in town. Drunkenness fuels social injustice against the poor in every age. Our society needs governmental officials who will refuse bribes and judge impartially. The underprivileged should be able to count on fairness in a courtroom. Drink demolishes this confidence.

Common decency screams, "Drunk driving destroys the lives of more than 23,000 people a year. Where are the laws to stop this homicide?" Common sense discerns the sad reality—the congressman who habitually drives home from parties drunk cannot be relied upon to vote to stiffen penalties for DWIs (those driving while intoxicated).*

My associate pastor served on the jury in a DWI case. As they deliberated in closed session, the evidence of the case glaringly portrayed the guilt of the defendant. He would lose his license, which was the required penalty at the time. One of the jurists began to argue, "Wait a minute! How is this man going to get to work? How will he continue to live a normal life? Which one of you hasn't had too much to drink at times? Remember this could be your neck someday!" My friend responded, "You have missed the point of this trial. If the defendant is guilty of breaking the law, he should face the legal penalty for this crime. The issue is not how this would affect our lives if we were facing the same judgment." The license was never taken away. The case stalled on a hung jury. Intoxication perverts justice.

My wife's fifteen-year-old brother was murdered by a drunk driver on New Year's Eve 1981. The driver who struck David down was driving without a license—he had lost it as a result of three previous convictions.

Time magazine recently exposed this crime-alcohol connection on our college campuses. They reported the findings of researchers from the Harvard School of Public Health who interviewed 17,592 students at 140 campuses. "The researchers declared that nearly half of collegians are binge drinkers who cause all sorts of trouble, from vandalism to attacks on classmates. At the schools where drinking was most popular, more than two-thirds of students had had their

*Known in many states as DUI (driving under the influence).

sleep or study interrupted by drunken peers. More than half had been forced to care for an inebriated friend, and at least a fourth had suffered an unwanted sexual advance. Alcohol plays a role in 90% of rapes and almost all violent crime on campus" (December 16, 1994).

The Anesthetizing Sedative

> Give hard drink to the person who is dying,
>> wine to someone experiencing the intense bitterness of
>> grief.
> Let them drink and forget their poverty, and become
> unconscious to their bitter misery.

(31:6–7)

Ethanol, the active ingredient in strong drink, effectively numbs the self-conscious. Like other tranquilizers, such as Valium® and Librium®, it influences the synapses between neurons, thus retarding neurological function. This includes the brain. Lemuel's mother did not understand the biochemistry of neurotransmitters nor that their inhibition causes exhilaration, loss of social restraint, slurred speech, distorted sensory perception, drowsiness, and blackouts. But she did appreciate the sedating value of alcohol for those facing extreme pain or terminal illness. Much as an oncologist gives morphine to the dying cancer patient, she counseled Lemuel to give alcohol to those experiencing intense misery. The tragedy in our culture is that, unlike Valium® and Librium®, which demand a physician's prescription, we sell alcohol along with Coke® and Dr. Pepper® everywhere from basketball games to convenience stores.

In contrast to other psychoactive drugs, ethanol does not target specific nerve cells. It penetrates cells at will, and when taken in large doses harms almost every organ of the body. Myocardial disease, high blood pressure, stomach ulcers, shrunken testicles, infertility, birth defects, mental retardation, immune system deficiencies, cancer, and cirrhosis of the liver are the persistent, deadly affects of over-drinking.

When a football teammate says, "Let's go out after the game. My older brother drove to the next county and got us a pickup of Coor's™," our sons need to see a mental picture of a jaundiced hospital patient with a malfunctioning liver worn out from processing gallons of booze, suffering chronic blackouts, dying ten to twelve years earlier than his or her expected lifespan. Our children need to know that the initiation to this condition began with, "Have a drink and prove you're a man!" A visit to the alcohol rehabilitation center at a local hospital and some interviews with recovering alcoholics could be some of the most effective training we give our children concerning the booze cartel in the United States.

I still remember a lesson my dad taught me as a five-year-old on a New York subway. His Saturday youth rally had gone late, as usual. It was about 11:30 p.m. when the doors electronically slid open and we boarded the subway. Immediately, the stench of the alcohol hit me. On the floor was an empty wallet and an unconscious drunk. His suit was expensive, but torn and soiled. Blood trickled from scrapes on his face. On the wall above his head was posted the latest beer ad, in which a knockout blond at the side of a bronzed muscle builder toasted ice-cold mugs and proclaimed the slogan, "Here's to Life!" As Dad knelt down to try to help him in, he pointed to the ad and said, "David, that's what the world says. This is what it is."

Modern pharmacology can offer sedatives without some of the potential hazards of ethanol for moments of extreme crisis. Any mind-altering drug taken in massive doses becomes poison. Those responsible for the good of others cannot afford to be slowly poisoned. God's children, like King Lemuel, are royalty. It will demand all our wits to be the "salt and light" Jesus desires us to be in a decaying society.

Sobriety will also save God's children from some of the rough effects of companions who regularly drink alcohol—brawls (20:1, 23:29), wasted resources (21:17), psychotic hallucinations (23:33), and confusion (23:34). While I was visiting a hospital recently, a doctor told me that more than 80 percent of the patients were there due to conditions caused and aggravated by alcoholism. It is our number-one drug problem and a close second to cardiac arrest as the leading cause of death in the U.S. Imagine hearing this news flash from Dan Rather *every night*, "Six hundred die in air disaster!" More than that die every day, either directly or indirectly from alcohol.

It sparkles in the crystal goblet and goes down dry and smooth. The alcohol companies sell the illusion it will transform you into a great athlete or a stunning "party animal." Proverbs tells the truth. In the end, it strikes like a rattlesnake. Its venom is more potent than a cobra's (23:31–32). How can we help our kids control this snake?

Controlled by the Spirit

Do not get drunk on wine, which leads to wasteful destructive living. Instead allow the Holy Spirit to fill you. (Ephesians 5:18)

Prohibition demonstrated that legislation cannot adequately control the human being's craving for the "spirits." External rules can never cage our intense passion to feel good, laugh with friends, and celebrate life. At the cocktail party, alcohol creates a euphoria and a freedom to socialize. The bar becomes a place to share deeply and find support from friends. This is Satan's counterfeit for the body of Christ. He substitutes a deadly drug for the Holy Spirit. We must not assign the evil to the chemical but to ourselves. We are committed to the lie that we can meet the needs of our hearts without allowing God to be in control.

The slanderer's deception continues as he turns our gatherings at church into boring dull lectures instead of Holy Spirit-controlled celebrations of forgiveness and family intimacy. When our children do not see us making music together and freely expressing our thanksgiving to God for the gift of His Son, they become prime candidates for the enemy's church—the club circuit. As they mature, our children must make the choice between living a life controlled by the "spirits" of alcohol and living a life controlled by the Holy Spirit of God. Again, we return to the individual's responsibility to decide who will be sovereign at the core of his being.

> You have spent enough time in the past doing what pagans choose to do—living in debauchery, lust, drunkenness, orgies, carousing and detestable idolatry. . . . The end of all things is near. Therefore be clear minded and self-controlled so that you can pray. Above all, love each other deeply, because love covers over a multitude of sins. (1 Peter 4:3, 7–8 NIV)

God's children are all aspiring for higher office. Let's beware of the Spiked Punch Bowl.

Think About It

1. Do you know a recovering alcoholic? Why not have him or her over for dinner? After the meal have this person sit down in the living room with your entire family and share his or her experience. Let the kids ask the questions after you get things going.

2. Jonathan, Joel, and I went to a Texas Rangers baseball game. All around us, quarts of beer were being consumed. One of the fans spilled his all over Jonathan. Later, a fight broke out, and a force of security guards had to keep it from exploding into a riot.

On the way home I asked the boys how they felt about all the drinks served at the ball park and the mixed messages about alcohol communicated. What are some of the situations your family has experienced with the problems of drunkenness? Listen to your children's feelings and thoughts about some of these.

15

Word Power

Tom Clancy's war saga, *Clear and Present Danger,* runs 656 pages long. Where do all those words in an author come from? We do not need to look far. The average American opens his mouth to talk approximately 700 times a day. This adds up to approximately 3500 words daily, which means we communicate the equivalent word sum of a Tom Clancy blockbuster every couple of months. Unfortunately, this pile of words does not guarantee we can weave together a mass of intricate, technical details into a riveting tale of espionage and war. We may not all be Tom Clancys, making millions on military-political adventures, yet Proverbs wants each of us to become an expert on the power of words, their limitations, their source, and the characteristics of wise word usage.

More important than mastering word processing on a computer is the need for our children to master word processing in their minds, as well as the ability to speak clearly to others. Wise verbal skills are a must for leadership. Harnessing this powerful flow from the mouth is the distinguishing mark of wisdom.

"We all stumble in many ways. If anyone is never at fault in what he says, he is a perfect man, able to keep his whole body in check" (James 3:2 NIV).

The Power of Words

Life and Death

Death and life—they are in the power of the tongue; those
who cherish words will eat their fruit. (18:21)

Winston Churchill used words to resurrect his nation and the
Allies. Hitler used words to commit national and personal suicide.
Like Smokey the Bear, who teaches our kids about forest fires, we
need to help them appreciate how words can be used to bring
warmth or waste. Because the wise individual realizes the awesome
power in a word, he falls in love with language, including the precise meaning of words, their emotional impact, and the exact timing of their delivery.

He recognizes that wise teaching revives others like a bubbling fountain or a nourishing meal. Correct instructions can protect others from deadly errors (10:21, 13:14). Wise words combat
the lethal weapons of a false witness in a courtroom by shooting
straight to the truth (12:6, 25:18). Like Daniel appeasing
Nebuchadnezzar's anger, the wise person knows that honest, reasoned speech can save lives (16:13–14; Daniel 2).

To Bruise or Ruin

There is a person who speaks without thinking like thrusts
from a sword, but the tongue of the wise brings healing.
(12:18).

Reckless words pierce personalities like sword thrusts (12:18);
subversive words crush spirits (15:4); and slanderous words destroy
friendships (16:27–28). Wicked, godless words burn down not
only personal lives but entire cities (11:9, 11, 16:27). Only wise,
truthful, gentle words can put out the fires. Words can bruise like
Mike Tyson's fists, but they can also soothe like a gentle nurse's
hands.

Gracious, kind words can lift a crushed spirit up from the pit of depression (16:24). The individual dying of thirst in a desert of difficulties comes back to life with unexpected good news (25:25). Remember the good news from Egypt: "Joseph is alive and well!" It gave his aged father, Jacob, the gift of a few more years of life (Genesis 45:27).

Counsel from the heart of a friend is the perfume of a relationship (27:9). Even when it smells more like antiseptic than perfume, the straightforward, honest rebuke of a friend is far better than the unexpressed devotion of a secret admirer (27:5). Our true friends will risk the relationship to tell us the truth. This is the friend who sticks closer than a brother (18:24).

To Reward or Ruin

A person who guards his mouth preserves his life, but the person whose mouth is constantly open, destroys himself. (13:3)

The callused hands of a carpenter bring him his living by building houses. The disciplined, skilled tongue of an orator earns his living by building lives. Effective speaking is the manual labor of a leader (12:14). Like the farmer who plows and plants, the communicator brings in his sustaining harvest with words (18:20). As a pastor, one of my major responsibilities is to communicate effectively the concepts in God's Word each Sunday morning. In a tangible sense, I put food on my family's table by the hard work of teaching with my mouth.

The private Christian high school I attended nearly three decades ago could not afford state-of-the-art microscopes or hundreds of histology slides. As a chemistry major in college, it took me two years to catch up on the technical data. Though my high school failed to excel in math and science classes, it did give me a training that has turned out to be far more valuable.

In the spring every student memorized a speech from a well-known orator. One by one, before the entire student body, we had to ascend the steps to the platform, put our hands down at our sides, and deliver the declamation. The best in the freshman-sophomore and junior-senior divisions competed for "top gun" disclaimer. This declamation contest, along with debate and the recitation of "readings," helped me to get over the fidgets and to focus on eye contact, audience sensitivity, and the thrill of moving a group with words. I am grateful for teachers in high school who made me speak before an audience.

I am also thankful for a dad who called on me at random for a word of public testimony in his evangelistic meetings. One afternoon my dad drove our family up to Plattsburgh, New York, to do a weekly television show. Usually, a special guest rode along with us.

"Dad, is your special guest meeting us up there?"

"No," he replied, and kept his eyes on the road.

"Are you going to give a message yourself?"

"No."

"Then what are you going to do for a half hour?"

He looked at three of us kids and said, "Interview you guys."

The cameras almost made me wet my pants, but every time I get up to publicly proclaim God's Word I am thankful for a dad who gave me the confidence to speak. Kids do not have to be put on TV to learn how to speak. There are children's Sunday school classes, AWANA clubs, daily vacation Bible schools, and a host of other opportunities for our kids to mature in public speaking. In Midlothian our teenagers perform dramas from Romans or some other book of the Bible for the Sunday morning worship service. Teenagers cannot complain about boredom in the Sunday morning worship when church leaders allow them the freedom to take part in it.

Our kids need to learn early—words can enrich others and feed your family. But the wrong words at the right time can ruin your career, such as Jimmy the Greek's racial slur during a public broadcast (13:3, 21:23). Words can reward, but they can also ruin.

The Limitation of Words

As Derek Kidner, the English commentator, has analyzed in his book *Proverbs*, the wise individual, unlike the sluggard, understands that words are no substitute for actions (14:23). They cannot alter the facts (24:12, 26:23–28, 28:24), and they cannot compel a correct response (17:10).

We exposed the sugar-coated glaze over the sales pitch of the con artist (chapter 6) and the incorrigibility of the Impenetrable Block (chapter 3). We parents are responsible for communicating these essentials before we send our kids into the world. But we must accept the limitations of our words.

Words cannot force them to accept our values. If we could compel our kids to respond, this would be brainwashing them, not teaching them. We would destroy their will, which makes it possible for our children to love God with all their hearts.

The Marks of Wise Speech

Like the distinctive cattle brand that indicates the ownership of prize, registered stock, here are the identifying characteristics that show that these words belong to a wise person:

1. They are honest and fair (12:22, 16:13, 24:23–26).
2. They are few, not many (10:19, 17:28).
3. They are humble, not boastful (27:2).
4. They are patient, not nagging or argumentative (17:14, 19:13–14, 25:24, 27:15–16, 29:9).
5. They are private and confidential, not gossipy, or slanderous (17:9, 20:19, 25:9–10).

6. They are careful, not hasty (12:16, 15:1, 18:13, 25:15, 29:20).

7. They are apt, not untimely (15:23, 25:11, 20).

Like an EKG, our words reveal the health of our heart.

The Source of Wise Words

Wisdom is found on the lips of the discerning,
  but a rod is for the back of those who lack heart. (10:13)

The person with "heart" or the ability to discern between right and wrong and between wisdom and foolishness speaks consistently with such moral character. The person without this core uses his or her mouth destructively and pays the consequences. In his commentary, *Proverbs*, F. Delitzsch quotes a Talmudic proverb that captures the reality: "That which a wise man gains by a hint a fool only obtains by a club." To control the tongue we must go to the source of our words—our hearts. When the tongue is connected with a heart committed to God and His wisdom, it speaks words of life, healing, and edification.

This heart listens carefully to instruction (19:20) and carefully weighs its words (15:28). Recognizing that when one sleeps with dogs he catches fleas, the wise heart does not choose fools (13:20), short fuses (19:19, 22:24–25), or boozers (23:20) as its companions. Jesus stressed this word-heart connection: "Out of the overflow of the heart the mouth speaks. The good man brings good things out of the good stored up in him, and the evil man brings evil things out of the evil stored up in him" (Matthew 12:34b–35 NIV).

The telephone rang at 9:45 p.m. "Dave, I think Don, Martha's husband, suddenly died this evening." Praying that this tragic news was only a rumor, I drove out to Joshua's second grade teacher's home in the country. The tears on the faces of her ten- and fourteen-year-olds immediately informed me that the news was not a rumor.

Joshua adored this teacher, and when a substitute took his class the next day, and the principal tenderly informed their class that they needed to pray for their teacher and her family in their loss, Joshua took it hard. That evening he prayed for his teacher. "Dear Jesus, Mrs. Wetzig is in the Castle of Despair like Pilgrim. She needs Promise to come and rescue her." When he finished praying he crossed his hands behind his head, looked up at the ceiling and said, "Daddy, it's a good thing we have a man like Jesus around. He's the only one who makes any sense." Joshua's words told me that he had paid attention to the video series on *The Pilgrim's Progress* at church, but more important, they revealed the condition of his heart.

Those words from John Bunyan's 1678 classic and from a second grader's 1989 insights were the comfort and strength I used to close the funeral service the next afternoon. Sometimes "word power" is discovered in the mouth of a child.

Think About It

1. I mentioned several opportunities my high school offered me to develop my speaking ability. What are some of the ways you are encouraging your children to learn to use words skillfully?

2. On page 195 we discussed the limitation of words. Think of some situations where you have heard someone talk but saw no action. What were the results?

3. Some of you have children who have chosen not to listen to your teaching or follow your desire to know and love Jesus Christ. They have followed the path of foolishness. How can Proverbs 17:10 protect you from false guilt about their behavior? How can what we learned about wisdom's continued desire to reach those who are straying give you confidence to keep praying?

16

God and Power Politics

November in the U.S. means Thanksgiving and turkey, but every two years it also means election day—that special day in a democracy when "the people" become the government for a few moments as they cast their votes. Our children need to be taught by our example and words about the importance of personal involvement in community, state, and national government. The hard statistical facts prove that evangelical believers love to lament the sad state of politics, but often fail to register and express themselves at the one time when personal convictions can make a difference. Two factors tend to keep us away from the voting booth—intimidation from secularism and our own misconceptions about politics.

Though they have been free to shape public policy for the last thirty years, the secularist cries "Foul!" whenever those who believe in God venture out into the public square. They argue, "Morality and spiritual values should be kept safely locked up in a private prayer closet and behind the walls of a chosen place of worship." Politics is about economics, power, and influence, not about beliefs and morals. As political campaign rhetoric intensifies and the "culture wars" flame, we must not allow this kind of talk to intimidate us or our kids. Take a look at these political issues:

"The laws are unwholesome and not necessary to the public good!"

"Judges have been chosen based upon the partisan will of a political leader who also decides their salaries and tenure of office."

"Taxes have been imposed upon us without the consent of the people."

"We rely upon the protection of Divine Providence, we mutually pledge to each other our lives, our fortunes, and our sacred honor."

Modern secularists might want to exclude those who talk about "good versus unwholesomeness" and "justice versus bribes." They may mock those who are unashamed to admit a foundational commitment to God, but before they laugh away these ethical and spiritual concerns, they need to reread the Declaration of Independence. The issues cited above were only a few of the "political concerns" that led to the founding of our representative government. Ethics and spiritual values have a long, legitimate tradition in our political process. The "new kids on the block" are not those who believe God's standards apply to daily matters, but those who try to legislate His absence. We must not allow intimidation from secular unbelief to steal away our right to participate in the political process. Tragically, a group of God's children almost forgot this responsibility as they withdrew from the public debate.

Politics—Unsavory Bartending, Gambling, and Prostitution

I was raised in evangelicalism before the ascendance of Jerry Falwell's Moral Majority, Pat Robertson's and Ralph Reed's Christian Coalition, and Beverly LaHaye's Concerned Women for America. Voting was our American responsibility, but involvement in politics was demeaned along with other unsavory occupations, such as bartending, gambling, and prostitution. It was drilled into my thinking that "a committed Christian could never be elected to public office. The only way to win was to lie and bribe."

On the other hand, we grieved over the tearing of the moral fabric of our nation and blamed much of this wreckage on the government. So the vicious cycle maintained itself—government was a place for godless manipulators; therefore the godly did not get involved in this arena. This guaranteed that the arena was often left only to those who rejected God and biblical morality.

The advent of the "born again" era through Jimmy Carter and Ronald Reagan, and the cry of the Moral Majority, "Back to our Judeo-Christian roots," made this former aversion to political involvement among religious conservatives seem as quaint as an Amish black buggy. Pat Robertson, a prominent evangelist, went so far as to resign his organization to run for president. Influential evangelical organizations went to Washington to set up headquarters so that anti-God legislation would not catch us by surprise. Today what politician can escape issues such as "Right to Life," "Prayer in Public Schools," and "Traditional Family Values"?

Evangelicals—those committed to America's first faith, the faith of our fathers—have re-entered the public life of our nation. It is about time! Our ultimate citizenship is in heaven, but this does not relieve our responsibility to be good citizens here on earth. The apostle Paul not only taught us to obey our government, but also "to be ready to do whatever is good" (Titus 3:1 NIV). In a democracy this demands participation on election day and continued responsible involvement in government the rest of the term. But as we flex our newfound political muscles, it is important to ask some fundamental questions. Who do we believe is ultimately sovereign over the affairs of men and nations? What are the Divine Ruler's concerns in the courtroom, the business office, the war room? Are there some universal principles for governing that He recommends? Let us allow Proverbs to teach us and our kids some political savvy. Its balance can protect us from worshiping the political system as "the savior" and from withdrawing from it as "the satan."

Righteousness does exalt any nation, and sin is a disgrace to any people (14:34). But what do "righteousness" and "sin" look like from the perspective of Proverbs? How does God interact with power politics?

The Ultimate Power over the Powers That Be

"The king's heart [the power of the government] is ultimately in the LORD's hand; He directs it like a farmer directs the water in his irrigation ditch—wherever He pleases" (Proverbs 21:1).

Kings, prime ministers, presidents—they may think they rule, but they must all bow before the ultimate sovereign—God. Governments, like individuals, must respect the Architect. He is the Author of the destiny of individuals and nations. Nebuchadnezzar, Alexander the Great, Julius Caesar, Charlemagne, Napoleon, Hitler, and Stalin all used to strut their stuff, but, though the tyranny of their reigns grieves God's heart and earns His retribution, none escaped the plotline He is writing. And observe—they are all dead.

Nations can pray to Marduk, the god of ancient Babylon, to Horus, the god of ancient Egypt, to modern philosophy's "ground of being," or to modern cinematography's "the force," but all people live in the time and territory of the biblical God. All nations are ultimately "under God" and, like individuals, they must give an account to their Creator. Governments that recognize this objective reality and obey His moral precepts receive His favor and blessing. Those who reject Him are eventually crushed by their fantasy that God can be ignored.

John Winthrop, the first governor of Massachusetts Bay Colony, understood this when he wrote these words before sailing to the New World on the *Arabella*.

"Now the only way to avoid shipwreck and to provide for our posterity is to follow the counsel of Micah: to do justly, to love mercy, to walk humbly with our God" (*A Model of Christian Charity* 1630). It is time for his *posterity* to remember that "obedience to God's moral standards exalts a nation, but missing His standards brings shame to any people" (14:34).

The principles presented in Proverbs are never limited to a segment of the American population called "evangelicals" or "born-againers." They cannot be sealed up in religious services like ancient artifacts in a museum. These standards were in place before any human government was instituted (8:22–30). Proverbs was a Jewish book hundreds of years before Jesus came, and, when He did come, He endorsed its statements. The foundation of government is to respect and revere God's sovereignty. Let's sketch out what some of His universal governing standards look like in a courtroom, in a boardroom, and in a war room.

Justice in the Court

Highly paid lawyers strut into court like movie stars, and in the power of their oratory the issue becomes high drama, not the objective evaluation of truth claims. What does the ultimate Judge think about all this word manipulation and theater?

He recommends that judges honor those who speak what is right. Truth, not word manipulation, is to be the issue at stake in the courtroom. "Kings [governing authorities, in this case a judge] take pleasure in honest lips; they value a man who speaks the truth" (16:13). He warns judges not to declare the innocent guilty or the guilty innocent. "These are the sayings of the wise: To show partiality in judging is not good. Whoever says to the guilty, 'You are innocent,' his constituency will curse him and nations will denounce him. But it will go well with those who convict the guilty, and rich blessing will come upon them" (24:23–25). He attacks courts where perjury and bribes undermine fairness. "A false witness will not go unpunished, and he who pours out lies will not go free" (19:5). "Do not exploit the poor because they are poor and do not crush the needy in court, for the LORD will take up their case and will plunder those who plunder them" (22:22–23).

We need to be deeply concerned about our culture where the line between theater and reality has become blurred; where the entertainment value of an O. J. Simpson trial becomes more important than the issue of whether or not he did in fact commit two murders; and where the tactics become the cunning manipulation of the media and the jury rather than a humble concern to get at the truth. The trial in California was not the next multimillion-dollar feature film from Hollywood. This was a murder trial. There were two dead human beings, shattered families, and the accused. We need to pray that courtrooms will become places of truth, not entertainment, whether or not the city is Los Angeles. Lives are at stake.

You don't need a degree from Harvard Law School to discern that values like truth, justice, impartiality, and objectivity should have a say in our courts. So when we go to the voter's box, we need to choose judges, and politicians who appoint the judges, who care more about these moral values than they do about BMWs, Wall Street stocks, and exorbitant fees. It will take prayer and all the legal acumen a man or woman can muster to flesh out God's principles of justice in specific court cases. If they believe in moral relativism, they don't even have a chance. Our children need to see dad and mom involved in bringing justice to the judicial system.

Reward and Compassion in the Marketplace

Political liberals naively seek to apply compassion in the marketplace, but they forget to award competence and diligence.

Political conservatives, on the other hand, realistically reward skill and hard work, but can forget mercy toward those in dire need. God is neither naive nor compassionless. He promotes diligence and skill but never forgets kindness toward the weak.

I traveled and lectured in Poland before the triumph of Solidarity and the crumbling of the Berlin Wall. I'll never forget the sage humor of an aged Polish gentleman who sat next to me at mealtime and told me jokes through a translator. Who could forget his tongue-in-cheek humor about the Communist party? "We pretend to work and they pretend to pay us." Or, "Dave, did you know that Adam and Eve were communists?" (This was a bit of theology they failed to teach me at Dallas Seminary.) He grinned, "They had no clothes, one apple between them, and thought they were living in Paradise." His laughter goes to the core of why the tyranny of communism collapsed around the world.

A ruling party cannot snuff out physicians, engineers, and other intellectuals like insects and expect to build a robust economy. Lenin forgot a simple principle from the Bible—the workers of the world deserve their wages and a nation cannot prosper when competence goes unrewarded and incompetence is not viewed as a disgrace (14:35; 1 Timothy 5:18).

Beware when a political candidate promises you "daily bread," "physical health," and "protection from disaster." God, not government programs, can keep these promises. When you deify your government, you will lose far more than tax dollars. You will lose your individual freedom.

Political conservatism cherishes the individual's freedom and remembers the power of the free market. It does reward investment and skill, but it must not forget to insist on honesty in weights and measures, in advertising, and in product reliability and safety. God insists on a fair playing field that follows the rules of decency and compassion in economic play. Scales need to be balanced and conformed to true standards (11:1). God gets angry when greed skims off an unfair profit (16:11). Without God's principles, capitalism also forgets compassion for the poor.

We must never gloat over the disaster of others (17:5). God is the defender of those in need. When we graciously give to those too feeble to help themselves, we actually make a loan to God. We can count on His repayment of His debts; He is never a security risk (19:17). If we fail to respond to the cries of the poor, someday we ourselves will cry and not be answered (21:13). Every form of exploitation must be condemned (22:22–23).

Children whose parents do not provide for them, husbands and wives who fail to keep their promises to one another, pornographers who make billions on the violent abuse of children, capitalists who make windfall profits on products that destroy the health of millions—whenever the powerful victimize the weak, God will ultimately bring repayment (Romans 12:19). When we apply God's proverbs, we will be protected from upper-class bigotry, which either fails to give to the needs of the poor—classifying all of them as "lazy couch potatoes wanting a handout"—or assuages its guilt over luxuries by making liberal handouts. Proverbs encourages generosity to the disabled but never forgets human dignity. Every honest person who works hard to develop his talents from the Lord should be rewarded for his efforts. "Those who could work, but don't, should miss a few meals" (2 Thessalonians 3:10). These are the commonsense convictions we need to model in our homes and look for in our candidates.

Patience in the War Room

The government that recognizes the Lord's rightful sovereignty will not depend upon its arsenal for final security. "There is no wisdom, no insight, no plan that can succeed against the LORD. The horse is made ready for the day of battle, but victory rests with the LORD" (21:30–31).

The military hardware has changed from battle chariots to F-16s and aircraft carriers, yet victory in battle is still finally determined by the decision of almighty God. Personally, I do not believe Scripture counsels nations to beat their swords into plowshares before the Davidic Messiah performs this feat and sets up His world kingdom in Jerusalem. Until that time Proverbs does stress that patient diplomacy should precede hot-tempered retaliation. "Better a patient man than a warrior, a man who controls his temper than one who takes a city" (16:32).

But when negotiation fails and mobilization must take place, the military man needs to be given the freedom to execute a battle plan that will ensure victory. He will need many advisors to succeed. "Make plans by seeking advice; if you wage war, obtain guidance" (20:18). "A wise man has great power, and a man of knowledge increases his strength; for waging war you need guidance, and for victory many advisors" (24:5–6).

Vietnam should have forever taught us that slipping half-heartedly into war without the commitment of the people and without giving the military personnel the freedom to execute a battle plan guarantees the multiplied loss of life, as well as failure.

Competency and Morality in the Assembly Hall

Government officials should move up the ladder of power because of their pure motives and their ability to express themselves clearly and graciously, not because of their Machiavellian pragmatism. "He who loves a pure heart and whose speech is gracious will have a king [or a president] for a friend" (22:11). "Through patience a ruler can be persuaded, and a gentle tongue can break a bone" (25:15).

As in the marketplace, competence should be recognized in the halls of state. Skill, not a party spoil system, should determine political appointments. "Many curry favor with a ruler, and everyone is the friend of the man who gives gifts" (19:6). "Do you see a man skilled in his work? He will serve before kings. He will not serve before obscure men" (22:29).

Involvement—The Responsibility of the Righteous

If all this sounds anachronistic and naive in the sophisticated world of today's Washington or our state capitals, it is not the ancient principles of Solomon that will bring the last laugh, but the ruinous stupidity of a modern relativism that has forgotten common decency and ignored biblical ethics. But these principles will never be heard in the court, the boardroom, or the legislature unless we who are committed to God and His instructions get out of our "evangelical ghettos" and get involved in public affairs.

A first step is to vote on election days, and before these dates of reckoning, in the heat of the political campaigns, we must not forget to be "peaceable," "considerate," and "humble toward all men" (Titus 3:2). This includes our involvement in politics. Slander and gossip will be used against us—it is a powerful political weapon—but we must remember that when the "Christian Right" picks up these weapons, we instantly become the "Unchristian Wrong!" Our kids will see the inconsistency. What they need to see is their parents picking up their responsibility to serve the common good.

When the godly remember their eternal citizenship in heaven, but also assume their responsibility as citizens on earth entire cities and nations prosper (11:10, 14). Paul instructs us to not only respect and obey governing authorities, but also to be ready to do what is good (Titus 3:1). As we take our rightful place in the American democracy, we must remember that the only lasting solution to the human condition of slavery to immoral passions is not better laws or social programs. It is the forgiveness and renewal that only the crucified, resurrected Savior can give (Titus 3:3–8). But the opportunity to tell this truth does not come to those who lock up the good news in church. It comes to those who get close to unbelievers, and this includes the world of politics.

We can make a difference. I have seen this difference in my hometown. In response to many unsupervised parties where drugs and alcohol were the main ingredients for the destruction of lives and property, some citizens banded together and encouraged parents to sign the following pledge:

I Pledge to Provide a Safe Home

- I will not allow parties or gatherings in my home when I'm not there.
- I will not serve nor will I allow youth under the drinking age to consume alcohol in my home or on my property.
- I will not allow the use of illegal drugs in my home or on my property.

The cover letter that came with the directory closed like this: "The key to the Safe Homes Program is for you to realize *you are not alone* in your ideal to have an alcohol/drug free community. Use the directory to meet people who have publicly taken a firm stand of non-tolerance and non-acceptance of alcohol/drug use by the young people in our community. Just think of the impact it would make on Midlothian if each of you encourage just one more family to sign the pledge! You can make a difference." The letter is signed Barbara Jackson, Chairman Safe Homes Project. Barb also founded our Sunday morning children's church and is a respected women's Bible study leader.

The Safe Homes Project was sponsored by REACH, Resources-Education-Action-Council-Helping. When George Raffield, a young undercover officer, was murdered by some high-school students in a field a few miles from our church, Vera Wofford decided to unite the resources of our town against illicit drugs and alcohol abuse. REACH was born.

Jaccie Vitovsky and her husband Ed founded an AWANA program for children. No couple could be more active in their church's activities, but this did not blind Jaccie to the need for first-graders in our public school to increase their literacy skills. She came up with the idea of getting dads to volunteer about an hour a week to come to the elementary school and listen to a first-grader read aloud for fifteen minutes. Sixteen dads volunteered, and the children would be picked at random until everyone had a turn. The teacher drew the first name and the child went for the special time of reading. At the end of the session the volunteer dad came to the teacher with moist eyes. The child had never been able to read to a dad. They had never seen their own daddy. Jaccie received a letter of commendation from the First Lady for her efforts in literacy and involving dads with kids.

These believers have not compromised with the world but are penetrating the world with the love of Christ. We are to separate ourselves from the world of evil—all that is hostile to God and His moral standards—but we must not be separated from the "world of people." Let's remember the beginning of our children's first memory verse, "For God so loved the world . . . ."

Think About It

1. As we get involved in local school boards, city governments, and state and national politics, what are some of the characteristics of the wise person's character that will give us skill in this arena? What kind of responses should we expect and how should we respond?

2. We live in a society that tells the Thanksgiving story without mentioning the Pilgrims' most important belief—their dependence upon God. The Easter bunny and eggs are welcome at Easter, but not the mention of the resurrection of Jesus Christ. What steps can we take to be sure that our children get the facts about the spiritual heritage of our country?

3. Family discussion: Should a believer think about entering the legal profession? If so, based upon what we have learned in this chapter, what should be the beliefs and attitudes that guide this involvement?

4. Are you registered to vote and do you take the time to do this in local, state, and national elections? It is disobedient to God's instructions to us about government for us not to be appropriately involved.

Conclusion

Our children grow up and cease to be children. My two older boys, Jonathan and Joel, have already flown from the nest. This is tough on us parents, but if we are wise, we won't resist this growth toward independence. When our kids walk out of childhood into adulthood, two women wait for them on the street—Lady Wisdom and Lady Folly. Proverbs 9 pictures this Main Street of life.

Lady Wisdom, as we have learned, seeks to turn their hearts toward God and His skillful principles of living. Earlier, she invited the naive teenager to fall in love with her and turn away from the demolition crew with its mocking, dullness, and impenetrability to spiritual values. She challenged the youth to reject self-destructive arrogance and humbly open his ears to her lectures on a commitment to the Architect and his views on money, sex, and power.

When the constraining net of parental authority slips away, it is time for our kids to reveal whether Lady Wisdom has won their hearts. In her home is warm fellowship with other men and women who have chosen the truth. Jesus promises that this fellowship will never end. It is an invitation to the eternal marriage supper of the Lamb (9:3–5; Revelation 19:9).

In flaming, seductive red, Lady Folly waits for our young adults as well. She loves those without a heart—without a godly, moral core. She promises incredible "highs" as her victims enjoy the release from "God's limiting restrictions." Forbidden fruit is the sweetest, she claims. Her home presents itself as a mansion full of delights, but it is all a deceptive facade. Her invitation is to a funeral, not a wedding. When you accept, you enter a morgue, a funeral parlor filled with the corpses of those she has already murdered.

As parents we cannot control the choices our children will make. We can, however, commit the core of our being to wisdom, illustrate the fruit of this commitment with our life example, and teach our children the facts of life. When it's time for them to walk down Main Street by themselves, we must allow them to decide whether they will enter the house of wisdom or of folly.

But on graduation day, we can rejoice when some have made the right choice.

The small town commencement processional was completed; all the graduates had taken their seats along with about two thousand guests; the salutatorian had completed her speech, and it was now time to hear from the valedictorian. He shuffled his papers and began:

"Well, here we are. We're at the bright light at the end of the tunnel; the moment we have anticipated the past thirteen years. And here I am (you see I have a talent for stating the obvious). As valedictorian I am supposed to give a valedictory, an address, a farewell. We are at a unique position in our lives. We have come to the end of our childhood. We stand at the edge of a cliff, about to leap into the black unknown, walk across this stage and fall into the depths of adulthood—the proverbial real world. But before this traumatic event, we have a few minutes to take a pause, savor the past, and say farewell to our first eighteen years."

The senior proceeded with the usual reminiscing about childhood, thanks to parents and teachers, and inside jokes about school experiences. Then he continued.

"All of us look back at our memory books and see happy times and tear-stained pages. We've grown up the past thirteen years and shared our lives. Although most of us can't wait to get out, this small town has been our home and a wonderful place to grow up. We look back and see that all along the way there have been people helping us get here. Our teachers do not receive the praise they deserve. We thank you for the years you have invested in our lives. I want to thank all of you, my friends, for sharing your lives with me. I thank my grandparents who are here tonight for the great family legacy and example of wisdom with which you have blessed me. I also thank my brothers and sister, but most of all, I thank my mom and dad. You have taught me to live. Thank you for providing a stable home, for loving and being faithful to one another. This is a priceless gift.

"The past is behind and now we look toward the future. We look, but what to our wondering eyes can we see? Nothing! None of us can see the future. We can only inch forward day by day like a blind man with a stick. Some of us will stay here and raise a family. Some will move away, far away. Some will start working, and others will start college. Some will strive to get lots of money, drive an expensive car, wear the clothes, have the house. Some will strive to be the most beautiful person they can be. Still some will go bald, others get fat, and sadly, some will grow senile with age. Each of us will live striving to find fulfillment. We will each choose to live for something that brings meaning to life.

"Most of you have seen the movie *City Slickers*. If you didn't, I'll fill you in on the basic idea. The movie is about three guys who have been friends all of their lives, just like us. They are all approaching forty and wondering what life is about. The three of them go through a typical midlife quest and start doing all kinds of adventuresome things for fulfillment. The movie starts with them getting chased by a herd of angry bulls through the streets of Pamplona. They end up deciding to take a two-week vacation driving cattle out west.

"In one of the scenes Curly (Jack Palance), the hardened old cowboy, a *real* man, takes Billy Crystal out to round up some cows. As they are riding along, they start to talk and Billy decides to ask the big question. 'Curly, what's the meaning of life?' Curly keeps riding, looks hard at Billy, and simply raises one finger. Billy persist, 'But what is it? What is the one thing?'

"Curly removes his cigarette from between his lips. 'It's the meaning of life—one thing! I'm not going to tell you what it is. You have to find it for yourself.'

"Before we graduate, I want to share with you my 'one thing.' The one thing I have decided will bring meaning to my life is to love my best Friend with all my heart. My best Friend is someone who loves me for who I am even when I hurt Him or desert Him. He is always there for me. Most of all He died for me. He sacrificed everything for me so that I could live. The one thing I will live for is Jesus Christ.

"As we say farewell, I want to share one final word. I stand before one-hundred-and-forty-six dreamers. All of you have goals and aspirations. Get rich, marry the right guy or girl, be successful. All of these things are good dreams, but they cannot bring the fulfillment you want. They all fade in time. I want to challenge each of you to find the one thing—the only thing which will bring you fulfillment—the person, Jesus Christ."

There was silence and then the cheers broke out—an intense standing ovation. That is the way our oldest worldly-wise but innocent son, Jonathan, finished his high-school career. He is now about to graduate from the University of Texas where, with his brother Joel, he has had the privilege of living for his ultimate friend, Jesus Christ, in the difficult battleground of the secular campus.

The week after Easter, last April, Mary and I received this note from Joel about what the Lord was doing at the university.

He writes, "Just last night we had a Concert of Prayer. Around five hundred students came out to be involved in a night of prayer and worship to kick off Resurrection Week. Our focus was unity, and we planned to have a time of personal and corporate confession, pray for unity among the body, and partake of communion, and then go on a prayer walk around the UT campus. But God altered our plans. As my friend prepared to lead the prayer time, God strongly convicted him about his personal sin and the need to confess, not only to God, but to his classmates. He obeyed and the Lord powerfully moved in the prayer service. For three hours, leaders of different Christian organizations confessed their critical spirit toward one another. Individuals confessed pride, divisiveness, immorality, and many other things that were destroying unity among those who had decided to follow Jesus. After experiencing this draining time of confession, we all shared communion as one body of Christ and then spent an hour lifting praise to our Lord and Savior. It was amazing. The most powerful time of worship I have ever had. I am excited to see what God has in store for our campus in the coming weeks. Love, Joel."

Testifying for Jesus Christ at a public high-school graduation and experiencing the strong wind of revival on a secular university campus—our kids can grow up, leave the nest, and go out and live for Jesus Christ in the public marketplace. More than twenty years ago, Mary and I studied Proverbs together and decided to build our home on these principles. God has graciously given us two young men who have joined us in this commitment to wisdom. Two middle-schoolers are still at home moving from naiveté to a committed choice to live godly lives in a godless world. Pray that our family will continue to choose to believe in God's wisdom. We pray God will move your children to join many in the next generation who are building their lives on the word of the ultimate Wise Man.

The foolish man built his house upon the sand.
The foolish man built his house upon the sand.
The foolish man built his house upon the sand,
and the rains came tumbling down.
The rains came down and the flood came up.
The rains came down and the flood came up.
The rains came down and the flood came up.
And the house on the sand went smash!
The wise man built his house upon the Rock.
The wise man built his house upon the Rock.
The wise man built his house upon the Rock,
and the rains came tumbling down.
The rains came down and the floods came up.
The rains came down and the floods came up.
The rains came down and the floods came up.
But the house on the Rock stood firm.

—*Ann Omley*

Note to the Reader

The publisher invites you to share your response to the message of this book by writing Discovery House Publishers, P. O. Box 3566, Grand Rapids, MI 49501, U.S.A. For information about other Discovery House books and music, contact us at the same address or call 1-800-653-8333.